Bears, Bears Everywhere!

SUPPORTING
CHILDREN'S EMOTIONAL HEALTH
IN THE CLASSROOM

Bears, Bears Everywhere!

SUPPORTING CHILDREN'S EMOTIONAL HEALTH IN THE CLASSROOM

Lesley Koplow

Teachers College, Columbia University
New York and London

Published by Teachers College Press, 1234 Amsterdam Avenue, New York, NY 10027

Copyright © 2008 by Teachers College, Columbia University

Library of Congress Cataloging-in-Publication Data

Koplow, Lesley.
    Bears, bears everywhere! : supporting children's emotional health in the classroom / Lesley Koplow.
        p. cm.
    Includes bibliographical references and index.
    ISBN 978-0-8077-4903-6 (pbk. : alk. paper)
    1. Early childhood education—Social aspects—United States. 2. Classroom environment—United States—Psychological aspects. 3. Child development—United States. 4. Educational toys—United States. I. Title.
    LB1139.25.K648 2008
    372.1102′3—dc22   2008019500

ISBN 978-0-8077-4903-6 (paper)

Printed on acid-free paper
Manufactured in the United States of America

15 14 13 12 11 10 09 08   8 7 6 5 4 3 2 1

Contents

Acknowledgments

I AM VERY GRATEFUL TO all of the teachers, principals and parents who supported this work by allowing practice vignettes and photographs to be shared in *Bears, Bears, Everywhere*. I am especially thankful for the unique contribution of upper-grade emergent curriculum that so powerfully illustrates the potential of integrating transitional objects into upper elementary school classrooms.

Introduction

THE CLASSROOM DOOR opens to 23 boisterous 5 and 6 year olds, each carrying a lunch box and a backpack, each bringing in a social story and some emotional issues that might not fit neatly into the cubbies with the coats and books. The children put their things away and settle into the classroom while their teacher watches with a mixture of relief and trepidation. Yesterday started out well enough, but as the morning went on, the classroom began to vibrate with social turmoil and eventually became flooded with emotional storms that interfered with the curriculum and disrupted the learning process. The teacher wonders how things will go today. She takes a deep breath and prepares to begin her morning.

The teacher and children in this classroom and in many classrooms across the country might feel a greater sense of well-being in the school environment if they were to include Teddy Bears in their early-grade classroom routines and curriculums. Initially, this idea may strike educators as wildly inappropriate or, at best, as a cute, potentially motivating gimmick. But including Teddy Bears in early-grade classrooms is neither frivolous nor irrelevant. Indeed, including them in the classroom process can give children a voice for fears, worries, and conflicts that sometimes underlie inattentive and disruptive behavior in the classroom. Bears in the room can help the teacher create a "holding environment," a place where children feel "held," even when they are struggling. This technique can help him or her build a foundation for a pro-social peer community within the classroom environment, setting the stage for more positive peer interactions and an emotionally safe environment at school.

In order to use the techniques suggested in this book, teachers have to, for example, create a physical and psychological space for 23 Teddy Bears to join the 23 children in the classroom for the balance of the school year (the number of bears should match the number of children). *Bears, Bears Everywhere!* will give the reader guidance for using bears as transitional objects (symbols for their attachment figures), as self objects (representations of emerging self concept), and as vehicles for inventing psychosocial curriculum that can address complex developmental issues within the classroom. This book is designed to give teachers a deep understanding of the rationale for using stuffed animals as part of the classroom process, as well as to provide a road map for implementing this technique as a way to help children feel safe, connected, valued, and well cared for in school.

Most importantly, having Teddy Bears in the classroom may relieve the teacher of the burden of trying to "teach around" the "elephants in the room" that distract children from their learning. These "elephants" are the many unresolved social and emotional issues that accompany children to school and often stem from difficult experiences elsewhere. Teddy Bears give teachers a way to acknowledge these emotional and social issues that are the result of disruption, loss, trauma, and confusing experiences in the lives of young children. When institutional denial allows these "elephants" to roam the halls unattended, children get trampled by the weight of the intrusion and the power of the early school years is threatened. Having Teddy Bears in the classroom can help educators acknowledge these "elephants" so that they become smaller, better integrated, and less disruptive to the classroom process. When Teddy Bears come to school, children and teachers may feel a greater sense of well-being, allowing receptive, energetic learning to take hold.

CHAPTER 1

The Art of Relationship, the Science of the Brain

ART AND SCIENCE

TEACHING HAS OFTEN BEEN described as an art as well as a science. Integrating Teddy Bears into classroom life engages the artist in the teacher, as well as the scientist. Many early-childhood and early-grade teachers are intuitively able to build deep relationships with their students and tune into their emotional needs. These teachers may participate in many strong relationships with children, but may not be familiar with the science of early childhood brain development, which illustrates the meaning of those relationships as a bridge to successful learning. Other teachers may approach subject matter with expertise but be unaware of the power of their connection to the children as they transmit their material. Brain research provides us with a mandate for integrating the art and science of teaching. It supports innovative practices that enhance the teacher-child relationship and addresses social and emotional developmental issues as a fundamental component of early-grade education.

MAKING CONNECTIONS

Healthy infants come into the world with ever-expanding intellectual capacities. As we watch infants develop into toddlers and toddlers develop into preschool children, it may seem miraculous that a young child can make so many connections so quickly. The 3 year old already has close ties to her parents and her preschool teacher, and is beginning to show increasing interest in the children in her peer group. She is delighted with herself as she discovers cause-and-effect relationships, generalizes her language learning, and persists in asking the adult why things happen the way they do.

While the developmental process can appear miraculous, science tells us that the extent to which a young child's innate capacities are able to unfold is an outcome of the interaction between a child and her relationship environment (Friedman, 2005; National Scientific Council on the Developing Child at Harvard University [NSCDC], 2007; Shonkoff & Phillips, 2000). A child's relationship environment is made up of the interactions between the child and the significant others in his world.

Research shows that after birth, children's brains develop in response to the attachment partner's (parents, siblings, teachers) engagement, attunement, mirroring, and touch, and continue to develop within the interactive context of relationships throughout childhood. From the beginning, neurons in the baby's brain are stimulated with each caregiving interaction. When supportive caregiving routines are repeated over time, the neurons send out synapses to connect with other neurons that allow the baby to make affective and cognitive connections between one experience and another. Simply put, researchers have found that positive adult-child interactions in the early years create affective connections in the brain, allowing the baby to make cognitive connections over time (Jaffee, 2007). The parent who mirrors her baby's distressed affect in an empathic way, with a parallel expression of negative emotion, creates a pathway for understanding the meaning of emotional communication in her baby's brain (Meltzoff & Decety, 2003).

While all healthy children are wired for learning, responsive interaction with early relationship partners is an essential ingredient for the learning process to thrive. Studies indicate that the quality of interaction with caregivers, teachers, and other adults who participate in the everyday lives of children also play a significant role in a young child's brain development (NSCDC, 2007; Watamura, Donzella, Alwin, & Gunnar, 2003). This role may be especially critical when children's relationship partners at home are unable to be involved, attentive, and consistently supportive. If a young child is unable to use his parents to develop emotional attunement and social learning, he may be at a loss in the school environment, which demands interaction and engagement. Indeed, the development of emotional attunement initially shown in the baby's ability to read adult affects for social and emotional cues is one of the earliest forms of communication and social learning and serves as a foundation for the development of reality testing as children grow (Beebe, 2004; Gibson & Walk, 1960). (Reality testing involves evaluating the environment and the relationship of the self to the environment; it is a way to know if the environment is safe. To do this, children depend on affective clues from adults and on their own physical explorations of the environment.) Without reality testing, children may be unable to keep themselves safe in school, to focus, or to master abstract concepts. Therefore, teachers who have perfected the art of the relationship are offering more than they may realize to children at risk. Not only are they offering empathy and emotional support; they are also offering pathways to the development of a social and emotional infrastructure that can help children move toward age-appropriate reality testing, an understanding of cause and effect, and the language of making connections.

COMFORT THROUGH EMOTIONAL STORMS

Infants and toddlers do not yet have the ability to regulate their own emotional responses. Infants depend on the comfort of a responsive adult in order to move through a tearful, rageful, or frightened state and regain some emotional balance. Infants' and toddlers' emotional storms are often powerful and, at times, overwhelming for the caregiving adult, as well as for the children themselves. While staying with very young children through emotional turmoil may be difficult at times, we know that it is important to pick up and hold a baby who is screaming and crying in distress. We know it is helpful to be present for the tantrum-throwing toddler in order to help her regain her emotional balance when the tantrum is over, and to talk about what she might do the next time she is frustrated.

When children are young, they depend on adults to help them survive negative affects without becoming overwhelmed by their own feelings or fears about their own destructive potential. With adult support, little by little, young children can learn how to communicate their distress in increasingly specific and effective ways, and to regain emotional balance after becoming upset. As they move into the primary school grades, well-supported children develop an increasing capacity for emotional regulation and assume the regulatory functions that were once only the province of the adult.

Children whose attachment partners are not able to help them regulate strong emotions or to tolerate their negative affects may not develop the capacity for emotional regulation by the time they enter school. In addition, children with developmental issues and delays may not have mastered this early milestone. This lack of mastery puts these children at risk in the school environment, where emotional storms are easily stimulated. It is significant that research shows difficulties with emotional regulation in preschool and kindergarten to be an accurate predictor of school failure in 4th grade (Hamre & Pianta, 2001).

STRESS AND THE DEVELOPING CHILD

All young children experience a certain amount of stress in their lives. Internal stress, such as being hungry, wet, cold, or too full, can upset the equilibrium of the infant or toddler, who is easily overwhelmed by physical discomfort. External stressors, such as loud noises, a family move, or an overcrowded environment, may also cause the infant discomfort. However, if these stressors are short-lived for a young child or ameliorated by an attentive, attuned adult, detrimental effects can be avoided. Indeed, short-term stress that alleviates quickly can promote growth as children move through the toddler period and enter the early childhood years. For example, the thirsty 3 year old who has to wait a couple of minutes before her mother can get her a drink learns that waiting results in a positive outcome if her needs are met sooner than later. The child experiences a short wait having positive results. Little by little, the young child who experiences benign, short-term stress begins to increase her frustration tolerance and learns to accept delayed gratification. However, if the thirsty 3 year old is frequently forgotten by a preoccupied adult and never gets his drink and must often go to bed thirsty, the stress can become overwhelming and disruptive to the developmental process.

Stress that is chronic, overwhelming, and not ameliorated by adults can become toxic to young children (NSCDC, 2005). Toxic stress comes from unrelenting and extreme stressors, including family and community violence, extreme deprivation, abuse, and neglect. This can have a devastating impact on the developing brain. Like adults, when babies, toddlers, or young children are overly stressed, their bodies release high levels of the stress hormones cortisol and adrenaline. These hormones allow people to take immediate action under stressful conditions, especially to avoid danger or attack. When cortisol and adrenaline are flowing, the ability to act instantly is enhanced and the ability to think deeply is simultaneously inhibited (NSCDC, 2005). Adults often describe their actions under stress as being automatic: "Without even thinking, I reached for the intruder's weapon and grabbed it from him." "I was running so fast I didn't even realize that I had passed the finish line until there was nowhere else to run." "When I saw the raccoon run in front of my car, I slammed on the brakes without even thinking about the traffic that might have been behind me." In all of these examples, the people involved were only able to think about the events once the stressful incident had passed and hormone levels had subsided.

When very young children experience chronic and toxic stress, high levels of hormones are released and become their physiological norm. When these hormones are stimulated too often, and stress remits too infrequently, levels do not subside but instead remain chronically high. This results in brain architecture that promotes impulsive, defensive action and diminishes the child's access to higher-level thought processes (Gunnar, 2003).

Thus, when highly stressed children enter the classroom, their bodies do not immediately adjust to the more protective environment, and the behavior that results from high stress hormone levels does not change quickly. When adults reprimand their impulsive actions, children may be at a loss to explain the cause and effect of what has occurred. When the school environment itself is also very stressful, the child's experience at school will reinforce her brain architecture and diminish her capacity for abstract thinking and receptive learning.

SCHOOL AS A HEALING FORCE

While some of the research cited may be alarming to educators, studies show that strong adult-child relationships can act as a buffer for toxic stress and alleviate ill effects over time. Teacher-child relationships have the capacity to be healing because teacher-child interactions take place over time on a daily basis. Stress hormone levels for children in supportive daycare centers were found to diminish after children recovered from separating from their parents, while stress hormone levels increased after separation in poor-quality centers (Watamura, Donzella, Alwin, & Gunnar, 2003).

Not only do relationships and supportive caregiving routines set the stage for the psychological well-being of young children, they affect their physiology and learning potential as well. While teachers have the power to affect their students in profound ways, they are rarely acknowledged for the critical role they play in the lives of their students.

Attuned, responsive teachers become partners in the development of the young children in their classrooms during the hours they spend together each day. This teacher-child partnership can be life-altering for children whose outside partnerships are not strong enough. Given that there are increasing numbers of young children who are difficult to maintain in the classroom due to impulsive, disruptive, or aggressive behavior, it is imperative that teachers be encouraged to take their relationships with children seriously.

Sadly, in the era of No Child Left Behind, teachers have been taken away from attending to the relationship aspects of their work and made to focus on improving children's performance outcomes on standardized tests instead.

Schools that heal are schools that remain focused on the relationship aspects of classroom life in spite of the political pressure to do otherwise. These schools know that they need to create climates that ameliorate stress instead of exacerbating it. Schools that heal find innovative ways to maintain stable adult-child relationships throughout all grades, and enhance the quality of caregiving routines. They weave emotionally responsive curriculum into their daily literacy, social studies, and art learning environments. Introducing Teddy Bears into the classroom process can be a powerful way to begin.

WHAT TEDDY BEARS BRING

Teddy Bears in early childhood and early-grade classrooms give children a way to symbolize their supportive relationships with their teacher. Using them allows teachers a way to humanize caregiving routines and to integrate emotionally responsive curriculum into the existing daily structure. Teachers invite Teddy Bears into the classroom to help children understand and express their own feelings in constructive ways and understand the feeling states of other children. They use bears to decrease stress and anxiety and to give themselves a vehicle for addressing unresolved developmental, social, and emotional issues that hinder children's socialization and learning processes.

Teddy Bears belong in 21st-century classrooms because leaving children alone with toxic stress or overwhelming, unregulated emotions is debilitating for them. Allowing young children to suffer social and emotional isolation without taking preventive action constitutes institutional neglect and puts children at risk for depression and antisocial behavior as they grow up. This is a risk our schools cannot afford to take.

CHAPTER 2

Transitional Objects Within the Holding Environment of the Classroom

HOW TRANSITIONAL OBJECTS WORK

IT IS NOT UNUSUAL for well-attached children to enter preschool or kindergarten with special blankets or stuffed animals tucked into their backpacks. During moments of distress, they may want to visit their cubbies for a reunion with these objects or may need to hold them as the day progresses. It is important for teachers to understand how well-supported children come to derive comfort from these special objects before creating a classroom that fosters their use.

Comfort objects, referred to here as "transitional objects," are typically invented by children during toddlerhood as they become increasingly physically separate from their parents. The toddler's newfound power to walk and run gives him the means to explore more of the environment and thus to venture farther and farther away from his parents. Toddlers experience conflict between the desire to be independent and their need for the security that comes from frequent contact with their parents. Since toddlers cannot yet internalize their parents when they are out of sight, many children resolve their conflict between the safety of staying close and the excitement of venturing out by inventing a symbol for the parental figure. Toddlers endow a teddy, blanket, or other soft toy with the symbolic capacity to represent the intimacy and protection of the parent-child relationship. This special object, which is called a transitional object, gives toddlers the connection to the parents that they need in order to feel secure until they are able to achieve object constancy (the ability to carry the parent internally in their minds). With a transitional object at hand, a child is able to go upstairs to play while her parent is downstairs. She is able to fall asleep in a darkened room. She is able to say "bye-bye" to her mother and stay in childcare while her mother goes to work. She is able to enjoy her apart-from-parents explorations of the world with the feelings of connection and freedom from anxiety that the transitional object gives her.

A child who invents and uses a transitional object has the foundations to accomplish many important developmental milestones. The existence of a transitional object implies relationship, because a child must have an attachment relationship in order to create a symbol for it. Therefore, a child who invents such an object indicates that both parent and child have become attached to each other. The invention of a transitional object also demonstrates the child's capacity to create symbols. Symbolic functioning is a precursor for language development, symbolic play, representational drawing, and meaningful reading and writing in the school years. Toddlers who use a transitional object are demonstrating the ability to solve problems symbolically. They are letting us know that they can follow the maturational pull toward increasing autonomy and still remain connected to the people they love. The preschool child who enters the classroom with one hand wrapped around her transitional object comes into the classroom with the capacity to connect and with the ability to invent her learning.

OBJECT CONSTANCY

Eventually, there is less and less need for the child to maintain contact with the transitional object as he develops his capacity to carry a comforting image of his parents internally. When a child is able to evoke a comforting image of his attachment partners apart from his actual contact with them, he has achieved the crucial developmental milestone of object constancy. With an "internal parent" to comfort him during moments of adversity in the classroom, the child is free to invest his emotional energy in activities that involve exploration, self-expression, social interaction, and symbolic play and learning. He no longer needs to use his energy worrying about reuniting with his parent or surviving other children's intrusions, and he is free to join his friends who are building a city with the blocks, pretend to be a firefighter in the dramatic play corner, or make something with Play-Doh. This child is now able to use symbolic play not only to represent his attachment relationship, but also to make sense of his life experiences by interpreting them on a scale that allows for integration and mastery.

WHEN CHILDREN DO WITHOUT

When children lack the secure relationship base that underlies the creation of a transitional object, they may come to school "doing without" some essential inner resources that are needed to thrive in a group setting. They may have difficulty separating from their parent, or using the teacher as a "home base" from which to explore the classroom. Without this ability, a child may be disorganized and disoriented at school and lack a sense of initiative in goal-oriented activities. Children who are older than 3 and have not yet achieved object constancy may be ill-equipped to cope constructively with adversity in the classroom. Frequently, children who are doing without object constancy act as though they are alone when difficulties arise. Without an internal source of comfort, they don't know how to look for an external source of comfort. They feel as though they must fend for themselves if they are to survive conflict or confrontation. When another child sits in her favorite seat, grabs her lunch box by accident, or says something unkind, the child without object constancy tends to take aggressive action. Such action may be extreme and is out of sync with the circumstances, but it feels necessary to the child, who is protecting herself from a perceived threat.

The child who does not have the relationship basis that underlies the ability to internalize a comforting voice is likely to experience rejection from teachers and other children, who become angry and frustrated by his behavior. This experience of rejection heightens his sense of worthlessness and emotional isolation, and deepens his conviction that he must act in his own self-defense (see Photo 2.1).

THE CLASSROOM AS HOLDING ENVIRONMENT

Teachers who address object constancy issues in pre-K through 3rd-grade classrooms may be using the most powerful form of intervention that can be made available to schoolchildren. Thousands of children come into public and private schools with unresolved developmental issues that hinder socialization and learning.

PHOTO 2.1. When children feel vulnerable,
they often assume a defensive, aggressive posture.

If we expect those children who feel unprotected and easily threatened to get along with their peers and focus on their learning, we are expecting superhuman powers from young children who literally lack "food for thought." Without opportunities for adult-child relationships that can support the early developmental processes of the psychological home base, transitional object use, and object constancy, children may remain at a loss in the school environment.

Schools that heal provide children with classroom relationships that can function as a psychological home base when children need one. Teachers in schools that heal enhance those qualities of the classroom that allow it to become a "holding environment" (Winnicott, 1971/2005) for the community of children within. This term refers to a safe, containing space that allows children to express both positive and negative affects in constructive ways. Teacher-child attachment relationships are encouraged within the holding environment of the classroom.The classroom process nurtures the development of a community where children feel responsible for one another, and it even includes children who are difficult to like.

Certainly, one of the qualities of the classroom that makes it a potentially powerful holding environment is the frequency of contact between its members. Classroom life occurs 5 days each week for 10 months of the year. Typically, children have the same teacher or teachers throughout the year and remain with the same group of children, giving relationships time to develop and deepen. Daily school and classroom routines have the potential to become containing, predictable, and grounding experiences for children who lack continuity in their home experiences. Consistent, supportive relationships and predictable, nurturing routines can give children a sense of their own worth and help them relate to school as a place they can count on.

Another quality of early-childhood and early-grade classrooms that lends itself to the development of a holding environment is the process of communication and self-expression that can be included within the curricular structure. To do well in developmentally appropriate early-childhood programs, children have to learn how to express their thoughts and feelings through play, drawing, group dialogue, writing, and project work. When orchestrated by teachers that heal, these activities become avenues for the children's development of symbolic capacities that can become a voice for their emotional experience. Such activities help children connect to one another, thereby diminishing their risk of emotional isolation over time.

The most powerful transformational quality of the early-childhood classroom is the teacher's authentic connection to each of her students. In order for children to "feel held" in school and to use their relationship with the teacher to strengthen object constancy, it is necessary for the teacher's affects, language, and actions to be genuine. If the teacher-child relationship is to become an integrative force in the lives of young children, the teacher must be able to connect with, empathize with, and contain both the positive and negative affects that her students express. This may be a difficult transition for teachers who were raised with rigid definitions of "right" and "wrong" and "good" and "bad." To help children integrate negative as well as positive experiences and emotions, teachers have to be able to allow for the constructive expression of both.

Teachers who heal refer to negative affects and emotions in context and help children build the bridge to thinking about social and emotional cause and effect. For example, when the assistant teacher leaves the room unexpectedly, the head teacher approaches a child who is pouting and refusing to join the group. She begins to verbalize the cause-and-effect relationship between her co-teacher's departure and this boy's behavior. For example, Ms. H may say something like, "Adam, I know it's hard for you when Ms. L leaves the room, but I also know that she will come back. Some kids have known adults who don't come back when they say they will, and that makes it hard for them to believe that the teachers will come back. But I am sure that Ms. L will be back soon. You can join the group, or you can sit down here and draw something about Ms. L."

In addition, the teacher can try to get the children to express themselves verbally when they are upset. For example, when a

Photo **2.2. Having a Teddy Bear brought comfort to this child, who could then relax and experience joy.**

child begins to scream after another child takes his toy from him, Ms. H reflects the negative affect back to the child by saying, "Jonah, I can tell you are angry and upset, because you are screaming. But I have no idea what happened to make you upset, or what to do to help you, because the screaming is not telling me the story of what happened." When children's negative emotions are reflected back to them in the context of their experience, they have a partner in the difficult job of making sense of their emotional lives (see Photo 2.2).

HOLDING THE TEDDY BEARS

The milieu of the classroom must be a strong enough holding environment to foster a comfortable and useful relationship between the children and their bears. The holding environment is *both* an essential ingredient for the introduction of Teddy Bears and a potential outcome of including Teddy Bears in classroom process; it is both a means and an end. For the reciprocal relationship between the bears and the environment to take hold, the classroom teacher has to endow the bears with meaning as self and transitional objects, and in so doing help them to "come to life." She must be comfortable acknowledging dependency needs in young children, and giving these needs a voice.

When teachers give children Teddy Bears as part of classroom life, the bears have the potential to become symbols for the security of the teacher-child relationship. The bears can help instill in young children the psychological freedom to move away from the teacher and take productive action in the classroom without feeling isolated, abandoned, or endangered. The bears may help children tolerate short separations from the teacher, such as the separation of resting during rest time, and may also be helpful for longer separations, such as the teacher's absence on a given day. Teddy Bears that are "held" as meaningful by the classroom teacher can help to ameliorate the stressors that may derail young children in the course of the school day (see Photo 2.3).

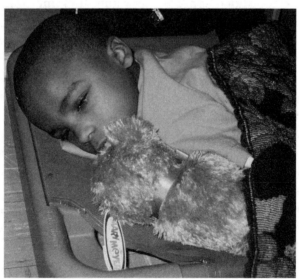

PHOTO **2.3. Having a Teddy Bear to hold
may allow a stressed child to rest.**

CHAPTER 3

Welcoming Teddy Bears in the Classroom

CHOOSING BEARS

EACH CHILD IN THE classroom should have her own bear; therefore, the number of bears will depend on the number of children in the class. Teachers may want to obtain additional bears in case children enter in the middle of the school year. The bears can be as small as Beanie Babies or as large as a 16-inch stuffed toy. Bears that are 8"–12" high with soft and flexible bodies are recommended, since they are big enough to cuddle but not so big that they take up too much space in the room. It is important that the bears be a generic variety—that is, that they come without a predetermined identity. Children need to "invent" their bears, name them, and be in charge of who they become. Therefore, bears that are representations of Winnie the Pooh, Paddington, Care Bears, and so on should not be used for this purpose. Teachers should look for bears that have a comforting feel and an appealing presence. They should have sweet but neutral faces so that children can project various affects at various times. Neither should bears with cartoon-like faces be selected, nor bears with the realistic features of wild bears. Most teachers find it easier to get bears in one neutral color, or at most, a few colors. Aside from color, bears should be identical or close to identical. The distinguishing characteristics of each bear need to come from the children's imaginations.

Bears are most often made from a plush material, but when allergies or asthma make that undesirable, terry cloth or soft cotton bears can be used.

INTRODUCING THE CHILDREN TO THE BEARS

While the classroom teacher who has selected and purchased bears may be tempted to give them out immediately, it is more powerful to introduce the bears gradually. Before each child is given a bear to hold, the teacher has to set the stage for the relationship between the children and the bears to unfold. Teachers need to answer some essential questions in their own minds before they give bears to their students. While using bears in the classroom is in part an improvisational art that responds to the issues that children bring to school with them, the teacher needs to clarify his initial goals for having Teddy Bears in the room so that he can communicate these goals to the children. He must ask himself, "What are the salient, common-ground issues that this group of children experiences that might be addressed through the bears? Knowing this group of children, how can the bears be introduced in a way that is contained and invites children to explore their relationship to the bears little by little?"

When working with bears in classrooms, I often recommend putting the bears on a high classroom shelf where children can see them and talk about them before actually interacting with them. The group process of preparing the children to receive the bears and integrate them into the life of the classroom is an important precursor to using the bears well. The following sample narratives from teachers who were introducing bears into their classroom process help to set the stage for the initial focus of the work in each classroom.

Introductory Dialogue #1

The kindergarten teacher has put the bears up on a shelf. At the beginning of morning meeting, she asks the children a question. (Please note that all children's names are pseudonyms.)

> *Teacher*: Has anyone noticed anything different about our classroom today?

Children: We have bears! There's so many Teddy Bears!

Teacher: What have you noticed about the bears?

Anna: They're not pushing each other off the shelf!

Teacher: You're right! They are not pushing each other, but kids in this classroom have been pushing a lot and doing other dangerous things to each other. The bears will stay in our classroom all year, but before we can take them down we have to figure out how to make a safe home for them.

Introductory Dialogue #2

Pre-K teacher (at morning meeting): I have noticed that some parts of our school day make some of the kids feel sad or worried. Can you think of times when kids feel sad and worried?"

Cara: When mommy leaves.

When nap time comes.

Yesterday when I fell down.

Teacher: I was thinking about those times, and I thought that having Teddy Bears in our classroom might help when kids are feeling sad or worried, so I bought twenty bears, one for each of you. [Teacher opens the closet so that kids can peak at the bears.]

Teacher: We're going to get to know our bears little by little. We'll get to know what each bear likes and doesn't like, and what each one needs to feel safe in school. That way we can make our classroom into a good home for them.

Keith: How will I know which one is mine?

Teacher: When we're ready to take the bears down, each kid can see which one feels special to him. Each of you can choose a bear that feels special to you. Then we will make each bear something special to wear so everyone knows which one is their own.

Introductory Dialogue #3

> *First-Grade Teacher*: [Directs children to look at the bears.] These bears all look the same, but you have some ways that you are the same as other kids and some ways that you are different from other kids. Maybe these bears are all the same in some ways and different in other ways.
>
> *Daniel*: My bear is different because he's allergic to milk.
>
> *Teacher*: Daniel's bear is allergic to regular milk, but might love drinking soy milk like Daniel drinks. To understand about being the same and being different, I wonder if you can think about ways that the kids in this class are the same and ways that they are different. (see Plate 1)
>
> *Children*: [Kids raise their hands to offer examples.] Some kids are different because they are allergic to things. That means they have to eat different things.
> We're all in first grade. That's the same.
> We all have you for our teacher.
> We're all in the Milestone School.
> There are some kids who are already 7. That's different because it's older.
>
> *Teacher*: Good! We're going to study the ways that we are all the same and the ways that we are all different for a while. When each of you gets his own bear, you can figure out how to help your bear learn what they have in common with other bears and also discover his own unique identity.

Introductory Dialogue #4

> *K/1 teacher* [expecting baby]: By now, all of you have noticed that there is a baby growing inside of me. That has made a lot of children curious about babies. Some children know a lot about what babies need when they

are born, and some children are wondering. I decided
to give each of you your own Teddy Bear to play with
while we are talking and learning about babies. These
Teddies will stay in the classroom with you all year
long, even when my baby comes and I have to be at
home. When you finish the K/one class, you can take
your Teddy Bear home with you.

Randy: My auntie had a baby yesterday.

Steven: I know how to take care of babies. I have two baby
sisters.

Lulu: Can we pretend that our Teddy is our baby?

Teacher: Yes. You can pretend anything you would like to
about your Teddy Bear.

Introductory Dialogue #5

Second-Grade Teacher: It has been such a scary time at our
school since the fire happened and burned some of the
places in our building that were important to us. I have
been thinking about what might help us to feel safer. I
bought some Teddy Bears for our classroom, enough
for each child to have one. I thought that having Teddy
Bears in the classroom might help us to feel safer little
by little.

Miguel: I want one! I want one!

Teacher: There are enough for everyone who wants one.

Peter: [Has been chewing his sweater and fidgeting] Can I
go to the bathroom?

Teacher: Yes. Also, you can tell me if it is too hard for you
when I talk about the fire.

Introductory Dialogue #6

Third-Grade Teacher: You know this has been such a hard
year since I had pneumonia and had to be out of school
for so many days. Ms. Z [the principal] told me that
when I need to be absent, school is very hard for you.

It gets hard for a lot of kids to behave and focus on learning. I've been thinking about that, and about what might help. I decided to bring Teddy Bears into the classroom to help kids feel better when I'm out. Maybe we can work on a way to help the bears help us to keep the classroom the way we like it, even when I am out.

Cindy: Can we get them now, or do we have to wait till you're not here one day?

Teacher: We're going to get to know our bears while we're all here together.

LISTENING FOR CHILDREN'S RESPONSIVE VOICE

It is important to give children time to take in the initial message about the bears and to respond to the message by making comments or asking questions. The teacher can listen carefully to what the children bring to the dialogue. Their comments and questions will reveal the ways in which the bears are meaningful to them in the beginning, and teachers can use that information to influence their agendas for using the bears over the long run. These initial responses may also alert the teacher to children who are experiencing conflict about using a bear and therefore may need to proceed cautiously. Consider the following remarks made by children after having been introduced to the idea of having Teddy Bears in the room:

"Can we keep them?"

"Where did they come from?"

"Are they also for boys or just for girls?"

"Are they real? Bears bite."

"Which one is mine?"

"I don't need a bear anymore. I used to have one but now my baby sister has it. It's only for babies."

"Mine's gonna be Superbear and save the other bears from the bad guys!"

These are familiar initial responses when presenting the idea of including Teddy Bears in classrooms of early-childhood and primary-grade children. The teacher of a given classroom listens to the children's reactive voices and makes note of the themes that emerge. She hears concerns and interest in many issues, including continuity, origins, gender, real versus pretend, power, possessiveness, fear of aggression, and conflicts around having dependency needs. She listens for these themes as the impact of the bears on the children is gradually revealed, and invites these themes to become more elaborate as children explore symbolic means for resolving their developmental issues.

RESPONDING TO THE CHILDREN'S VOICES: MAKING THE CLASSROOM SAFE FOR BEARS

Consider the introductory narratives presented earlier. In the first example, the kindergarten teacher lets the children know that the bears will stay on the shelf until the children figure out how to make the classroom safe enough for them. This information elicits responses from individual children that the teacher must listen to and facilitate a group dialogue about in order to engage the whole classroom community in the challenge of accommodating the bears. The following is a sample dialogue that the teacher moderates after her initial introductory explanation about the presence of the Teddy Bears and the need to make a safe environment before taking them down from the shelf:

> *Children*: They *will* be safe!
>   Yeah, we will keep them safe!
>   Yeah!
> *Teacher*: How will you keep the bears safe when it's hard
>   for you to keep yourselves safe and to keep one
>   another safe?
> *Children*: [Pause.]
> *Deidre*: I'll keep mine in my desk so nothing can happen to it.

Rhonda: No! You can't do that! It's dark in there. He'll be scared!

Anthony: I'll write a big sign that says "Don't Touch" near mine.

[A child who has been sitting quietly raises her hand.]

Teacher: Yes, Chrystal?

Chrystal: We can make rules for them.

Children: Yeah! Rules!

Teacher: What do you think the rules should be?

Kaitlyn: Don't stomp on your bear.

Michael: Don't stomp on no one else's bear.

Deidre: Don't throw your bear around.

Craig: Don't let your bear hurt another bear.

Teacher: [Has been writing down the rules as the children suggest them.] Those are good rules. I am thinking about the classroom rules, which are also good rules, but the kids don't always follow them and children do hurt each other a lot. We'll have to do a lot of thinking and talking and planning about the things beside rules that can make our classroom safe enough for children and Teddy Bears.

Analysis of Kindergarten Teacher's Response

This kindergarten teacher knew that she wanted to begin her work with the Teddy Bears by focusing on social interaction and the establishment of a safe classroom environment. She sets the stage for this theme during the initial group conversation, which focuses on having the bears in the room. She lets the children know that they will work on this slowly and thoughtfully. She also knows that she will help the children to use the bears to voice and explore their emergent themes of power, fears, competition, aggression, possession, and conflict about growing up as the year progresses. She keeps in mind that new themes will probably emerge and need to be dealt with as the work continues.

WORKING WITH CHILDREN'S RESPONSES:
COPING WITH A FIRE AT SCHOOL

The following dialogue followed the second-grade teacher's introduction of the Teddy Bears as a way of emotionally healing from a fire in the school building.

Gene: I have a Teddy Bear at home.

Wendy: Ms. T, I had a Teddy Bear when I was little and we had a fire in my apartment and my Teddy died in the fire.

Teacher: [Ms. T is surprised, and takes a minute to respond.] That is a really sad story. You had a fire in your house when you were little and a fire at school. You lost a Teddy Bear in the first fire, and now you are getting a Teddy Bear because of the school fire. You must remember a lot about what happens when there's a fire and how it feels to lose something special.

Wendy: [Nods.] I might be a firefighter when I grow up, or work for the Red Cross.

Gene: I didn't want to come back to this school after the fire. It smelled bad.

Flavia: Me either! I didn't want to come back either!

Luke: I was afraid we might catch on fire ourselves!

Sammy: I was afraid the firefighters might come back and chop the door down like they did there when we had a fire.

Teacher: It sounds like a lot of kids are still feeling afraid. I'm going to hand out the bears, and you can hold your bear while we talk about what happened when our school had a fire and what kids are still worried about (see Plate 2).

Analysis of Second-Grade Teacher's Response

Although the second child who reacts to the content of her teacher's introduction to the bears has a frightening story to tell, her teacher stays with her and doesn't try to diminish the intensity of what the girl's experience was. She is able to reflect her experience back to her, and this allows the dialogue to continue with other children chiming in about their fears about returning to school. While the teacher could have provided reassurance in response to the children's comments, she chose to invite the conversation to continue by distributing the bears to offer comfort while discussing something frightening that affected all of the children in the classroom as well as herself and the rest of the school community. In this way, this teacher diminishes the risk of children being emotionally isolated, which might follow this community trauma if the children were not encouraged to make it a shared experience.

WORKING WITH CHILDREN'S VOICES: RESPONDING TO A TEACHER'S ABSENCE

After Ms. L, the third-grade teacher who introduced bears in the context of her frequent absences, discussed including bears in the classroom, the children participated in the following dialogue:

Cindy: I don't think the substitutes will like the bears. I don't even think they like us.

Terrell: Yeah, Ms. L. The last sub said she didn't care about the way we usually do things. She wants to do things her own way!

Teacher: Thank you for telling me that, Terrell and Cindy. Ms. Z and I care very much about things going the way you are used to in the classroom when I have to be out. I think Ms. Z and I have to have a meeting about that and about how to communicate what we want to happen here to the substitute teachers.

Gabe: I have a good idea, Ms. L. We can make a list of the important things for subs to know about our classroom. Include us having the Teddy Bears.

Teacher: Great idea, Gabe. Let's do it now. I'll be the scribe. What should we put on the list?

Analysis of Third-Grade Teacher's Response

The third-grade teacher validates the children's perceptions by listening and not contradicting them. It is quite possible that the substitutes do not enjoy the group of children who often act out their distress over the absence of their teacher. Ms. L also gets information that she didn't have before, about the nature of the substitute's communication to the children and the lack of continuity created by the sub's negative approach. She wants the children to know that it is important to her and to the principal that the routines of the classroom be respected. This teacher knows that in the long run, if she is successful in improving the quality of life in the classroom even when she is absent, things will go more smoothly. She is encouraged by the children's receptivity to the bears and their desire to include them as an item on the "how things should go in our classroom" list.

Comforting Words for the Teacher

There are many ways to use Teddy Bears in the classroom. Sometimes Teddy Bears allow teachers to explore issues that would otherwise be difficult to address. Teachers who are trying to address difficult issues within the group for the first time may initially feel ill at ease or out of place, just as teachers who are using Teddy Bears in the classroom may feel awkward about introducing an unconventional social learning tool into an educational climate that is driven by performance anxiety. They can take comfort in the knowledge that they are reaching out to children who may not have another adult to help them connect to and integrate difficult situations.

Teachers who give bears to children in their classrooms can take comfort in the knowledge that they are providing a symbol for hope and relationships that some children may not otherwise know. While teachers may fear that they will "do it wrong" when engaging in social and emotional dialogues, they can be secure in the knowledge that they are taking steps to decrease emotional isolation and reduce stress in the school environment, an intervention that is heavily supported by various studies. Indeed, to "leave well enough alone" may be engendering the biggest risk of all.

CHAPTER 4

Every Bear
Has His Story

NAME AND AGE

AFTER THE BEARS HAVE been introduced as a concept, given a context for use, and become a visible presence in the classroom, the teacher can begin to allow the children to interact with their bears. He may choose to hand them out, allow the children to identify the one that feels special to him before presenting it to him, or have bears in a bag or basket where one by one, each child can take his Teddy. Each child should be given a few minutes to explore and get to know her bear. During this initial interaction phase, it is important for each child to engage in the process of inventing his bear's identity. *What is this bear's name? How will we recognize him? How old is this bear? Where did your bear live before he came to our school?* The teacher extends these questions as part of the initial process for all age groups and for all contexts of classroom use. Each of these essential questions deserves time for reflection, discussion, and action, so that the children can answer in a meaningful way.

Children need to think before giving their bears names that they will have as long as they stay in the classroom—and probably longer. The process of naming can be studied as part of this initial period. How did the children get their own names? Were they named after someone? What do their names mean? How will each child choose her bear's name? What does the name mean to her? Inviting children to consider these questions about themselves as they invent their Teddy Bears fosters awareness of the meaning of their own life stories and allows these stories to become sharable within the context of the classroom community.

FIGURE **4.1. Child's writing.**

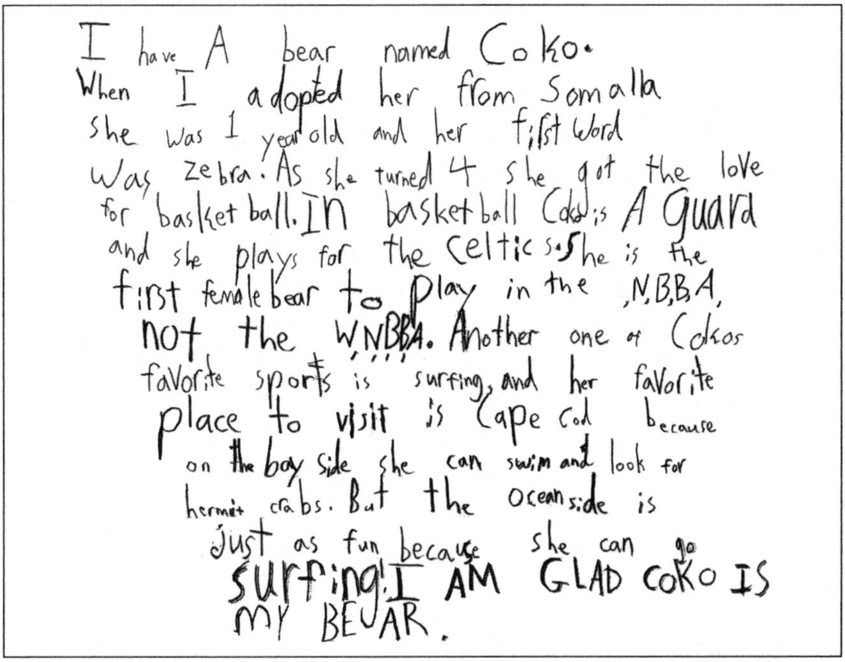

I have A bear named Coko.
When I adopted her from Somalla
She was 1 year old and her fi$t word
was zebra. As she turned 4 she got the love
for basketball. In basketball Coko is A Guard
and she plays for the Celtics. She is the
first female bear to play in the ,N,B,B,A,
not the WNBBA. Another one of Cokos
favorite sports is surfing, and her favorite
place to visit is Cape Cod because
on the bay side she can swim and look for
hermit crabs. But the Oceanside is
just as fun because she can go
surfing. I AM GLAD COKO IS
MY BEUAR.

Likewise, defining the Teddy as belonging to a certain age group helps children to communicate something important about their past, present, and future in an inventive and symbolic way. Asking children to invent the Teddy's history prior to joining the classroom communicates to them that their past experiences are valued at school and can be talked about and represented symbolically. As children think, talk, draw, play, and write in response to these questions, their own life stories become part of the narratives that they are creating for the bears (see Plate 3 and Figure 4.1.)

DISTINGUISHING FEATURES

Helping children to give their bears identifying features so that one bear can be distinguished from another is an important activity for all classrooms that are using Teddy Bears. Children can make collars and headbands for their bears by stringing different colors and patterns of beads, or can decorate colored ribbons to tie around the bear's neck. They can make clothes with different patterns and textures of cloth and Velcro, or booties with the same. Creative teachers can decide on age-appropriate ways to differentiate the bears. As the children participate in this process, the teacher may simultaneously want to develop a parallel focus on differentiating the bears by defining their likes and dislikes. What makes each of their bears happy, sad, angry, or afraid? What makes them worry? Which day of the year will be the bear's birthday? If children want to celebrate their bear's birthday, they will have to decide whether to make Play-Doh cake or real cake. If the bear wants other bears to make birthday presents for him, all the other bears will have to know what he likes and what he dislikes.

As children are invited to differentiate and define their Teddy Bears, they are learning to differentiate their own affects, passions, and dislikes, and to listen to and take in those of the other children in the group (see Photo 4.1).

PHOTO 4.1. Children enjoy the process of making a bear their own.

Рното **4.2. Making bears and their beds more personal
helps children differentiate self and other,
and promotes attachment to the bears.**

A PLACE TO BE

Teddy Bears in the classroom need a place to be when they are not in-volved with the children. While it can work to use children's cubbies, closet space, or shelves to store Teddy Bears, it is preferable to have each child make a safe space for her bear prior to storing him. I sug-gest using shoeboxes that children design according to their bear's needs. Making the boxes into cribs, cradles, beds, or houses helps develop the bond between the child and her bear as she works to create a comfort zone for him. Teachers can provide paint, markers, construction paper, flannel, glue, felt, and other materials that lend themselves to the activity as well as invitations to elaborate on the themes that are salient for the group. If children are making beds, the teacher might have materials available for sewing small pillows to put in them. She may remind kids that sometimes Teddies don't like to be in the dark alone and may like to have something to hold on to. Making a blanket for a bear that has symbols to help her feel safer at night is frequently one of the tasks that children are asked to accom-plish in their initial work with the Teddy Bears (see Photo 4.2).

The process of making a special place for bears invites children to think about the role of such places in their own lives. The teacher's invitation to make a safe place for the bear can be followed by invitations to talk about and create symbols and metaphors for safe places kids have or wish for, as well as stories about nighttime fears or dangerous places. By extending these invitations to talk, draw, write, and create with regard to a range of emotional experiences within the containing context of the Teddy Bear project, the teacher communicates her availability to connect to the child's world and hear her story. The process of listening to children's own stories with interest and empathy, and offering children opportunities to elaborate on their stories in meaningful ways, helps to facilitate and deepen teacher-child attachment relationships and provides the foundation for the Teddy Bear's use as transitional object.

EVERY CHILD HAS HER STORY

Children often feel that their own life stories are paramount. These stories are most often told at inopportune moments in early-childhood and early-grade classrooms. When asked to comment on a movie about bicycle safety, the young child raises his hand to tell about the time he rode his bicycle to the park down the street and it got stolen. When given a chance to comment on the classical music assembly she just attended, a young student raises her hand to say that her hamster died yesterday. When asked to read a story about a boy and his dog, another child bursts into tears and tells the teacher that his dog ran away last week. In many such incidents, children are often reminded of the subject at hand and told to keep their stories to themselves for the time being. The promise to "talk about that later" frequently does not materialize in the busy classroom. Because young children often fabricate or borrow material that is not their own, teachers may not always be sure if what they are being told is true. If the story is true, however, teachers may be unsure of the best way to respond. Given that their goal of the moment is about something else, they frequently move away from the child's own story, treating it as an unwelcome intrusion.

When children are behaving in an inappropriate or disruptive way, teachers may engage a social worker in the building to speak with their parents and find out what is happening to cause the negative behavior. Indeed, engaging the parent as a partner in understanding the child's life story is an essential intervention. However, whether or not the parent is available for this partnership, the teacher may be overlooking another source of gaining understanding. This source lies in the stories that the child himself tells outloud, through his play, in his drawings, and in his dictations and writing. All children need to tell their stories whether or not they are invited to do so. Working with the bears may sensitize teachers to this need, and may help new teachers make room for the children's narratives about their life experiences both as part of the Teddy Bear project and outside of it.

The following comments emerged in the context of the Teddy Bear project in pre-K and kindergarten classrooms, allowing children to tell some of their life experiences that may be difficult for them to master. For example, Adam, holding his Teddy Bear, raises his hand in his kindergarten morning meeting to say the following:

Adam: I wish I could take my bear home every day, but I might forget him when I'm at my Dad's house, and then when I'm at my Mom's house, I might be sad.

Teacher: Does anyone else want to tell a story about worrying about leaving something behind or losing something and wishing you had it with you?

Samantha: I have two houses too! Once I left my special pillow at my mom's house and I cried because it was my turn to sleep at my dad's.

Dannica: I left my lunch box on the school bus last week, and my mom said, "You'd forget your head if it wasn't attached on!" [giggling all around]

Teacher: Sometimes it's hard to remember where all your important things are, especially if you have two houses like Adam and Samantha do, or if you have a lot of places to go on the same day.

Jonah: I go to afterschool every day, and when it's all done,
   I ride on the school bus and I get so sleepy that one
   time I felled asleep and I missed my bus stop and
   the driver said, "Wake up!" in a loud voice, and I got
   scared!

Adam: [looking concerned] Then did he take you to your
   house?

Jonah: Yeah. My mom yelled at him because I was crying.

Maya: My mom yelled at the bus driver one time because
   he comes too late to pick me up and it makes my mom
   late for work.

Teacher: I'm glad we decided to keep our bears in school
   until the end of the year, so the kids won't have to
   worry about keeping track of them outside.

The comments and life-experience stories that were told in this group gave the teacher information about the nature of her students' experiences apart from the school setting. The stress of keeping track of their belongings or of themselves when they are only 5 years old is apparent as the children tell the stories of their busy and sometimes complicated lives.

Some of the children in Ms. C's kindergarten class depend on many environments to sustain them throughout their day. This knowledge helps Ms. C. to become more aware of the need to help these children build bridges between those environments so that they feel more connected, less preoccupied, and can become more receptive, secure learners. These stories also helped the teacher to understand the meaning of some of these children's behaviors and respond in more empathic ways.

TEACHER–PARENT–TEDDY BEAR

Parents of children older than pre-K may be curious about the presence of bears in the classroom and may need an orientation to the project along with other orientation information that is given to families at the beginning of the school year. During the orientation meeting, the teacher or school principal should mention that the children will be receiving Teddy Bears to keep in the classroom as part of their school experience. The principal can explain that the Teddy Bears are a useful way to foster positive relationships in the classrooms, and to help children have a voice for their thoughts, feelings, and experiences. Since bears are part of the school's academic program, they need to be present in the classrooms every day. The teacher or principal can let the parents know that each child will be able to bring her bear home at the end of the school year.

If parents are concerned about the bears or express resistance to the idea of including bears in classroom life, it may be helpful to do a parent workshop that involves some parallel experience. Allowing parents to have their own bears for the purpose of the workshop often helps to demystify the process and lets parents feel more comfortable with the project.

Teddy Bears in the classroom invite children to own their life experiences and communicate about them at school. The bears also offer children a vehicle for working on unresolved developmental issues that may impede learning. Since the Teddy Bears help children know the value of telling stories and the power of using symbols and metaphors to tell those stories, and also provide them with a source of comfort, it is important that parents know that everyone's stories are valuable as well, and that school staff can be a source of comfort during times of adversity. There are many ways in which to communicate the value of personal and family stories to parents. There are also many opportunities for schools to offer comfort to families in times of need.

Schools that heal communicate the value of stories throughout the school year. During the first half of the school year, all parents need to have invitations and opportunities to tell their children's important life stories to teachers if they feel it will enable them to better understand their children (Koplow, 2002). While most schools use parent-teacher conferences as a vehicle for the teacher to communicate classroom functioning to the parent, schools that heal use these conferences as an opportunity to gather important stories of children who have difficulties talking about their experiences in direct or accurate ways. Parents can be an important source of information when teachers are trying to make sense of children's unusual or difficult behavior in the classroom. While some parents may hesitate to share their children's personal or family stories, others will welcome the opportunity to help the teacher understand their child. Teachers may resist the idea of inviting parents to tell about their child's history. They may be afraid that parents will not want to talk, or will feel intruded upon. However, this technique has been tried in numerous urban schools where teachers have been surprised at how many parents welcomed the opportunity to connect with teachers in this way.

Beyond story gathering, parents can be invited to participate in expressive arts projects that give them the opportunity to represent child, family, and intergenerational connections symbolically. For example, quilt-making projects that include a representational felt square from each family, photo journals, and other hands-on projects can be integrated into an active parent-participation program in early-childhood and early-grade school programs, giving parents an ongoing experience that enables them to understand the power of symbols in facilitating communication and connection.

CHAPTER 5

Bears as a
Bridge to Literacy

LITERACY AND WELL-BEING

THE FACT THAT EARLY literacy development has become pervasive and greatly emphasized in our country over the last 10 years often serves to focus teachers on the use of specific teaching methods while neglecting the importance of engaging the whole child in the learning process. Yet there is much evidence that supports the value of addressing the whole child along the road to emergent literacy. Vivian Paley's well-known work in preschool and kindergarten classrooms highlights the ways in which children's dramatizations of their own dictated fictional narratives can facilitate personal growth, group process, and literacy development in young children (Nicolopoulou, McDowell, & Brockmeyer, 2006; Paley, 2004). Follow-up studies on Paley's story-acting technique with Head Start children found that the technique significantly improved decontextualized oral language skills and literacy awareness in participating low-income children (Nicolopoulou, McDowell, & Brockmeyer, 2006). In addition, researchers found that the children who dramatized made more frequent use of dictation and drawing journals and had more elaborate narratives in their journals than peers who did not attend classrooms with Paley's story-acting curriculum (Nicolopoulou, McDowell, & Brockmeyer, 2006). For many children, letter recognition, word walls, and decoding skills are the building blocks of literacy, but active learning and social and emotional integration are the mortar that holds the building blocks together.

As children grow into the early school years, literacy and mental health become increasingly dependent on one another. In order to become joyful and skillful readers and writers, children have to be relatively free of internal and external stressors that take their cognitive energy away from academic learning. In order to free cognitive energy for academic learning, children have to be able to express worries, fears, and other negative emotions in a variety of ways. When children are between the ages of 2 and 6, this kind of self-expression is achieved through verbal expression, symbolic play, representational drawing, and dictation. When children are between the ages of 6 and 12, the self-expression is achieved through verbal expression, symbolic play, representational art, and written expression. If written expression does not become a vehicle for conveying and integrating complex ideas, feelings, and experiences, children are deprived of an avenue that promotes self-reflection, communication, and connection. My prior work indicates that when children are able to create metaphors for complex emotional issues, they are less likely to become preoccupied with those issues or experiences and more able to devote energy to taking in and retaining learning (Koplow, 2002, 2007). In addition, children who can communicate about difficult issues in representational drawing and in their writing are less likely to suffer emotional isolation, as they are able to convey the nature of their experiences symbolically.

When children do not read at their appropriate age level and cannot write fluently beyond the 1st grade, they may experience loss of self-esteem and feelings of inadequacy that inhibit positive socialization at school and result in defensive behavior with peers and teachers. Therefore, not only is literacy an academic milestone; it is also an essential avenue of communication and self-expression that facilitates emotional well-being as well as expands cognition as children grow.

There is much support in both the educational and mental health communities for facilitating story-writing that includes children's imaginary and true stories as part of school curriculum. Indeed, Lucy Calkins's popular "Writer's Workshop" strategy encourages journaling and the development of personal narrative in young

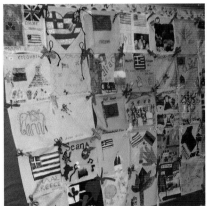

Plate 1. Teachers do activities that help children explore ways in which they are alike and ways in which they are unique.

My bear is afraid of things under the bed.

Plate 2. Some children use bears to express feelings that are hard for them to own.

Plate 3. Children express their thoughts and feelings through play, drawing, dictation, and writing.

My bear's name is Mama but he is still a boy. He is 6½ years old.

My bear's name is Ana just like me. She is a baby. She was sleeping during the story.

Something Special About me

I went to New York.

Something special about my bear. Her birthday is tomorrow.

Plate 4. Children use bears to explore identity issues.

Plate 5. Sending bears home helps children build bridges between home culture and school culture.

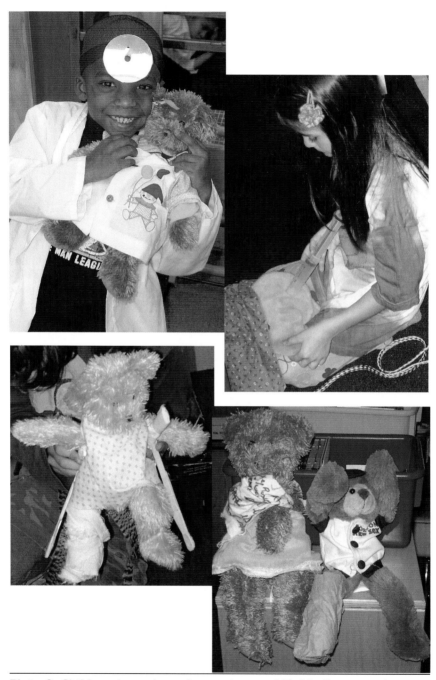

Plate 6. Children throughout the grades used Teddy Bears to play out themes of hurt and healing.

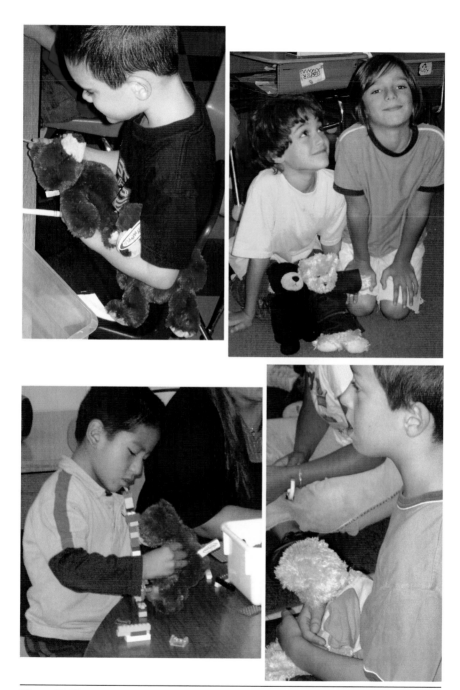

Plate 7. Teachers reported that the use of Teddy Bears in the classroom was especially powerful for boys, who may not have had other invitations to become attached to a comfort object.

Plate 7. (*continued*)

children's writing. However, the writing process sometimes seems out of reach for very young children, children who have trouble sitting at a desk and focusing, children with poor motivation, and children who need to move and be active in order to find learning meaningful. Implementing the Teddy Bear Project in kindergarten and early-grade programs can act as a bridge to literacy for these children as well as provide inspiration and security for those children without academic challenges.

PLAYING WITH TEDDY

As prior chapters indicate, using Teddy Bears in the classroom involves pretend play skills. Children "invent" their bears by giving them an identity; a history; and their own interests, feelings, thoughts, and passions. They play with them, care for them, and use them for company and comfort. The symbolic functions involved in using Teddy Bears in the classroom help children feel connected to who they were at younger ages, navigate the challenges of the here and now, and fantasize about who they want to be in the future. This helps them connect past, present, and future both cognitively and emotionally, and gives them a wider perspective that allows them to better connect to similar themes in literature and to write from these different perspectives when they become writers.

Since the bears are given to the children so that they can become meaningful and the children are given many avenues for expressing the meaning that their bears have for them, children learn to look for meaning in school activities and expect school experiences to be meaningful as they go forward (see Plate 4).

SYMBOL FOR A SYMBOL: DRAWING TEDDY

Literacy demands that children appreciate and create symbols that hold meaning. When children are experienced symbolic players, they have mastered the art of allowing one thing to represent another. For example, two children pretend that a small doll is the baby sister in their play, or that an orange juice bottle is a rocket ship. The two children playing have had siblings born recently whom they seem to feel would be much better off in outer space! This kind of symbolic play enables the development of symbolic thinking, giving children a hands-on way of creating a language that can capture and communicate complex and developmentally meaningful themes. The play that they create together captures their common experience and allows them to communicate with one another about it. Schools that heal invite children to participate in early-literacy activities that capture and symbolize their developmentally meaningful themes, heightening their intrinsic motivation for learning and allowing them to communicate their experiences in increasingly abstract ways.

Once children have established relationships with their bears and have had time to give each of them an identity and a differentiated appearance through dressing them up with clothing, being invited to draw pictures of their bears brings another level of complexity to their learning. When a pre-K or kindergarten child draws her bear, she is making a symbol of a symbol: She is creating a representation for something that already holds emotional meaning for her. When a child says aloud captions for his drawings, he is using language to capture and symbolize thoughts and perceptions. As he watches an adult write down his words, he observes a process of conveying spoken language into print and having the printed word hold the meaning of what he has been drawing and thinking about. This can be a motivating and intriguing experience for the young child who is embarking on a quest to find meaning in the written word (see Photos 5.1 and 5.2).

In a kindergarten class at the Miller School, the children sit with their Teddy Bears in their laps. The morning message asks the children whether their bears have a secret. All the children are invited to read the message out loud with their teacher. The class talks about the secrets that their bears have. Another child says his bear has a secret treasure in his closet. Another says that his bear threw his brother's toy in the toilet and is keeping that a secret. Then the

PHOTO 5.1. The kindergarten classroom integrated Teddy Bears into the social studies and literacy curricula.

PHOTO 5.2. This child dictates his journal entry, which accompanies the drawing of his bear's secret

student teacher reads a story about a bear who had a secret. The children are then asked to make an entry in their bear journals by drawing, dictating, or writing about their own bears. The following scenarios help to illustrate the ways that Teddy Bears act as a bridge to reading and writing for these children.

Nicky's Bear

Nicky picks up his bear enthusiastically and begins to interact with him. He holds him up to his face and rubs noses with him. He cuddles him and shows him to the kid sitting next to him. When another child drops his bear to pursue his journal writing, Nicky picks it up and nurtures it along with his own bear. Nicky then goes to the table to find the spot where his bear journal waits for him. He holds the two bears in one arm and draws with the other. His teacher notices that she has rarely seen him so focused. Nicky draws a representation of his bear, himself, and a large face with teeth that partially superimposes itself on the other images. When asked about the face, Nicky replies, "That's my face and my teeth. See? I fell and my tooth got hurt, and the dentist took it out because I have more teeths underneath and my other teeths will fall out soon anyway." Nicky is clearly anxious about this. His tone of voice is intense and he is very insistent that the teacher examine the place in his mouth that he is referring to. "What about your bear?" asks the teacher. "Will he lose his teeth and get new ones?" "NO!" answers Nicky emphatically. "My bear will keep his teeths in his mouth forever." The teacher offers to write the story of Nicky and his teeth, and Nicky gladly accepts the offer and is very attentive throughout the process. He cuddles his bear and his "foster bear" as he watches. "You will not lose your teeth," he says directly to his bear.

Miguel's Bear

Miguel, who has had his bear for a couple of weeks, has been able to give his bear a life of his own from the beginning. Miguel's kindergarten teacher suggested that the children choose a bear that "speaks to them." Miguel listened carefully as the bears were being chosen. When a child who had a turn before him chose the bear that Miguel had his eye on, he protested, "Hey! That's the one that was speaking to me!"

When a visitor came into the room to observe on the day that the children were working on their bear journals, Miguel approached her and asked, "Hey, are you gonna talk to my bear, or what?" The observer knelt down to meet Miguel's bear, "Ki Ki." This satisfied Miguel, who then tentatively approached the task of creating a journal for his bear, which most of his peers had already done. They were involved in adding drawing and dictation. Miguel's teacher reports that Miguel is not drawn to activities that require sitting for any length of time. Therefore, the bear journal was challenging for him.

First, Miguel sets his bear down on the table so it can "see" him at work. He laboriously colors a large representation of Ki Ki for the journal cover. Exhausted by his effort, he sighs with relief and brings it to show the observer. "There. That's Ki Ki. Now, take a picture of me and Ki Ki and my other Ki Ki that I drew," he demands. Once Miguel is able to see the image of himself, his drawing, and Ki Ki in the photograph, he connects to his accomplishment with enthusiasm. "Teacher! Teacher!" he shouts, jumping up with his drawing to where his teacher is sitting. "Look at my Ki Ki that I made *solito*!"

Elizabeth's Bear

Elizabeth sits down immediately when encouraged to begin her bear journal. She puts her bear, Kiara, on the table and begins to draw. Totally focused, Elizabeth creates an elaborate fantasy scene using the prompt on the morning message board, which asks the children if their bears have a secret. After working for a long time, Elizabeth gets a teacher to write down the story that goes with the picture of Kiara's secret. Kiara's secret is that she has a magic star that makes all her wishes come true. Elizabeth watches with interest as her teacher writes the words. She then writes her own name at the top of the page and Kiara's name in small letters on the bottom.

*   *   *

Each of these kindergarten children are within the normal range of comfort regarding activities that involve reading and writing for 5 year olds. Each child demonstrates her developmental level in the way in which she approaches the material and implements a given activity.

Miguel experiences a great sense of achievement after being able to represent his bear pictorally once he realizes that he has accomplished that. He is able to share this achievement with his teacher and with his bear, Ki Ki.

Nicky goes a step beyond the initial representation and adds a symbol for an issue that has been bothering him. He uses his bear drawing and writing to address and represent the meaning of the disruptive and worrisome experience of injuring and then losing his tooth. He then makes his bear represent a less vulnerable position that he wishes was his own.

Elizabeth endows her bear with the secret wishes that 5-year-old girls often fantasize and play about. She is able to use Kiara to create a fantasy that she can then symbolize in a detailed drawing as well as a complex narrative. In this way, Elizabeth's experience with her bear journal as an introduction to literacy communicates the potential of reading and writing to become a vehicle for expressing her own dreams, fantasies, and wishes.

READING TO BEARS IN THE EARLY-GRADE CLASSROOM

Bibliotherapy is the process of using literature to reflect and explore social, emotional, and developmental issues that are meaningful to a group of children. Teachers and school-based clinicians who do bibliotherapy as a classroom intervention choose books for read-alouds that reflect the common issues of the children in the classroom. They follow these read-alouds with group discussion and activities that invite children to express their own thoughts and feelings about the content of the stories. Bibliotherapy within the context of the Teddy Bear Project can be an effective tool for helping children become socially and emotionally attuned to themselves and their classmates, as well as engaging children in a form of literacy that involves their transitional objects.

Bibliotherapy can be especially useful when unexpected or difficult events have affected either a classroom community or an entire school community (see Chapter 9: "Bears in Bad Times"). Many teachers have found it useful to read to their children while they hold their Teddy Bears, who then become "listeners" along with the children. Teachers often ask children for their own thoughts and feelings in reaction to the story, but also wonder about how the bears feel about what they have heard. Often, children who have difficulty expressing their own reactions are able to attribute their feelings and comments to their bears and feel more comfortable acting as the "bear's voice" (see Photo 5.3).

The following anecdote may help the reader to understand the advantages of including bears in the bibliotherapy process.

A 1st-grade teacher, Ms. R, has been concerned about peer dynamics in her classroom. The children seemed to be getting more competitive with one another and less accommodating. While boys and girls had sometimes played together in the beginning of the year, by December a great divide had developed that Ms. R found difficult to deal with. Groups of boys and girls were taunting each other with "Girls Rule, Boys Drool" and "Girls Go Home and Suck Your Thumb." Ms. R's children had gotten Teddy Bears in late September, and while they had initially played an important role in the classroom, Ms. R realized it had been a while since she had initiated any Teddy Bear–focused activity. She decided to invite the bears to morning meeting and announced that she wanted to read a story to the group.

Ms. R chose to read Crosby Bonsall's *The Case of the Hungry Stranger*, a classic series for this age group about the adventures of kids who pretended to be detectives, but wouldn't accept kids of the opposite sex into their play. When she finished the book she said, "Does this book remind you of something?"

"Us!" several children responded.

"How does it remind you of yourselves?" Ms. R pursued.

"The girls don't want to play with the boys," Annica offered.

Photo 5.3.
4, 5, and 6
year olds need
invitations to
express feelings
about peer
issues.

I feel mad when my friends leave
me out.

"The boys won't let the girls in their club," Max explained.

"Why do you think that happens?" asks Ms. R.

"Because girls have cooties," says Devon. The boys laugh.

"Devon, we're having an important discussion. I notice your Bear Donte is listening respectfully, and I expect you to do that too."

The kids become quiet.

"I have noticed that in September boys and girls thought it was fun to play together, but recently, boys and girls are acting as though they are on different sides of the fence, or different teams. Do you know what I mean?"

Max raises his hand. "I want to say something. Some of our bears are still very small. Tiko is still five years old. Sometimes he really wants to play in the art area, but he's afraid the other bears will laugh at him because mostly girls play there."

Michaela raises her hand. "My bear Brownie is a girl, but when I first got Brownie, I decided Brownie was more like a boy but now I decided to make Brownie a girl again."

Ms. R says, "How did Brownie feel about being like a boy, and how does Brownie feel about being like a girl again?"

Michaela responds, "Brownie liked being a boy, because he liked pretending that he was a baseball player on the New York Mets team. Now Brownie likes being a girl because she likes to be with other girl bears and she wants to wear the rainbow bows I made for her."

"So Tiko and Brownie are not so happy with not having permission to sometimes play with both boy and girl bears and share some of their interests with each other. Are anyone else's bears unhappy with the ways that our classroom has been handling boys and girls playing together?"

A few other kids raise their hands. A few kids nod, or nod their bear's head.

"Let's think about this, and figure out ways to make the classroom more comfortable for both girl bears and boy bears. You can write some ideas down in your bear journal, and we'll try to be very sensitive this week when the bears are playing, to see how they're treating each other and how they are feeling."

The process of using bibliotherapy with her 1st graders and their bears allowed Ms. R to address a sometimes difficult classroom dynamic in an engaging, gentle, and thought-provoking way that gave the class a reference point for interactions between boys and girls in the coming days and weeks. Children readily allow their bears to voice their ambivalence about gender roles and boy–girl interactions, but have difficulty addressing these topics directly. Many of Ms. R's 1st graders were able to use their bear journals to follow up on this topic in writing. The reading, writing, and subsequent dialogues allowed Ms. R to refer to the content of these discussions when classroom dynamics surrounding gender issues became difficult. Talking in this way gave the children more perspective and more motivation to a pro-social approach toward one another.

WRITING ABOUT TEDDY

One of the most popular ways of encouraging children to write about their bears is through the use of blank books or journals. An example of this technique can be seen in the Teddy Bear backpack project that has become popular in pre-K, kindergarten, and 1st-grade classes across our country. Classrooms that include this activity usually have only one Teddy Bear in the classroom who goes home with each of the children for 1 or 2 weekends during the school year. Children write about the Teddy Bear's adventures in their own homes and neighborhoods, and then share the content of the Teddy Bear journal with their teachers and classmates. Often, parents of pre-K and kindergarten children become involved in the journal-writing with their children, and the Teddy Bear's visit becomes a way of engaging the whole family.

Another way of inviting children to write about their bears is by making books or journals for children to use spontaneously to write about their bears as well as giving children the opportunity to write about the experiences that the Teddies have at school (see Plate 5).

WRITING TO TEDDY

Being invited to talk, make pictures for, and write to their Teddy Bears often appeals to children who become attached to their bears as alter egos and confidantes. This approach may be particularly compelling to 1st, 2nd, and 3rd graders who may like the idea of having a place to write where they can express their feelings and tell their secrets to a nonjudgmental audience. They may appreciate the opportunity to write to their bears, similar to how older children are interested in writing in diaries (see Figure 5.1).

FIGURE **5.1. Third graders used their bears to inspire journal writing and fantasy.**

February 16, 2007

My bear is going to make an igloo over vacation. She is going to use chunks of ice and snow that I cut from the driveway. My bear Josephine said that she will make it big enough for me and my sister and her. She asked me to help her carry the big and heavy chunks. When the igloo is finished we will go inside it and tell stories. We will also drink hot coco. It will be fun!

Lisa

5/14/07

My bear lied about stealing Skittles from a store because he did not want to get in trouble. I lied to a friend that I thought my brother was weird because my friend thought my brother was weird and I didn't want my friend to not like me.

Randy

11/20/06

Dear Fluffy,

Yesterday in music we played a song with different instruments. There was a man named Tony and I don't know his last name. There were drums, shakers, bells and a Zilaphone. Tony picked us to play the different instruments. I really wanted to play the drums but I volunteered to play the bells instead.

When we played all together it sounded cool. It was also very loud. I liked it very much except it was just a little bit too loud.

Maxie

THE SECURITY FACTOR

Contact with comfort objects can be calming to anxious children, children who cannot sit still, and children who have concerns about their ability to perform "well enough." While holding their special Teddy Bear, or sitting with their Teddy on the table, anxious children may feel calm and secure enough to participate in activities that support emergent and unfolding literacy. "When I ask my third graders to read out loud or write something, sometimes anxious kids become almost frozen with performance anxiety," explains one 3rd-grade teacher. "When I ask them to read to their bears, or help their bears to write something, it frees them from the anxiety. It's really magical for a lot of kids."

This teacher's analogy captures the sometimes amazing effect that comfort objects can have in the classroom. The effects might seem magical for some children, but they are very real. The power of attachment as a facilitator of symbolic processes in infancy and toddlerhood is well known (Koplow, 2002; Winnicott, 1971/2003). Transitional objects that symbolize self and important others can still be comforting and inspiring to early-grade children who are crossing many bridges to more independent functioning and more performance-oriented schoolwork. Crossing the bridge to literacy with a Teddy Bear in hand can provide a safe passage for emergent readers and writers.

Bears in Pre-K and Kindergarten: Working with Developmentally Salient Themes

HAVING BEARS IN pre-K and kindergarten classrooms gives teachers a vehicle for helping children continue to work on unresolved developmental issues that may be interfering with learning and socialization. For instance, 4 and 5 year olds may enter school without the experience base to have achieved good self and object constancy, strong child-adult attachment, or the ability to use adults as a psychological home base. Without these developments in place, pre-K and kindergarten children are at a loss to cope with the routine transitions and separations that are part of the school day, and may be ill equipped to survive the many moments of adversity that occur in group life. The responsive pre-K and kindergarten teacher can give children another opportunity to resolve and strengthen these unresolved issues by weaving these themes into existing curriculum and by providing supportive routines and supportive teacher-child interactions.

In addition, pre-K and kindergarten teachers can use bears in the classroom to help children explore and address more age-appropriate developmental issues such as peer rejection, competition for power, and vulnerability to feelings of powerlessness. Pre-K and kindergarten teachers may wish to use literacy, social studies, and an arts curriculum to explore these themes using the Teddy Bears. Here are a few sample activities that demonstrate how teachers can use Teddy Bears in the pre-K and kindergarten classroom.

NEW PLACES, NEW TIMES

Objective: To acknowledge how hard it can be to adjust to new places, routines, and people. To help facilitate adjustment at the beginning of the school year.

Strategy: Children are encouraged to help their bears understand and adjust to the routines, transitions, and environments that comprise the school day.

Book for read-aloud at bear meeting: *I Am Not Going to School Today,* by Robie H. Harris.

Post read-aloud conversation topics: What did you think about the story? What did the story remind you of? How do you think the first day of school was for the little boy in the story? Why was he worried that school would be a confusing place? I wonder if your bears feel confused about things at school sometimes? What times of day are confusing for your bear? What do you think we can do to help our bears feel better during those times? How can we make it less confusing for them? How can we make sure they know when things happen at school, and how to get to all the important places?

Activities that support exploration of topic:

1. Children make picture schedules (which use drawings and photos instead of, or in addition to, words) of things that happen in the classroom routines for their bears.
2. Children and their bears engage in a school study. They take a walk through their school building to show their bears where all the important places are.
3. The children and their bears interview people who work in their school about what they do in their jobs. They take photographs to make a book for their

bears about the important places and people in their building. The focus is on places where the kids go during the school day (cafeteria, library, nurse's office, etc.), and places where the teachers go when they are out of the classroom.

4. Children make "my school" books for their bears using photographs and captions that they either write themselves or dictate aloud to the teacher. The books are available for children to read to their bears.

5. The children have a discussion about how the bears feel when they have to leave the room without them (e.g., to go to gym). They talk about ways to help the bears feel comforted when they are out of the classroom. The teacher writes their suggestions on easel paper as they speak. The children follow through by planning for and implementing the ideas that they come up with.

6. The teacher reads a story about a fire drill. The class discusses fire drills as a way of practicing what to do if there is a fire. Kids are invited to talk about what they know about fire drills. They need to understand about it so they can explain to their bears that they don't need to be afraid when they hear the alarm, but that the children will have to go outside quickly, and they will be back in a little while.

BEARS MAKE A WISH

Objective: To invite children to formulate, articulate, and represent their wishes. To help children connect to and express the need to feel powerful in a creative and pro-social way.

Strategy: Children are asked to attribute wishes to their Teddy Bears, and represent these wishes in drawing, dictation, writing, play, and acting. They are given the choice of trying to help make their bear's wish come true. If they choose to do this, they need to figure out which steps they can take to help make the wish come true.

Books to read at bear meeting: *I Wished for a Unicorn,* by Robert Heidbreder; *Stanley and the Magic Lamp,* by Jeff Brown.

Post read-aloud conversation topics: What did you think about this book? Does it remind you of anything? Do you make wishes sometimes? Can wishes come true? How do you make wishes come true? Does your bear have a wish? If she does, see if she will whisper it to you. Some people might want to share their wishes or share their bear's wishes. Some people and some bears may want to keep their wishes secret for right now. Does any child or any bear want to share a wish right now? What do you think about _____'s bear's wish? Do you ever have the same wish?

Activities that support exploration of topic (to be done over time):

1. Draw a picture of your bear's wish (in your bear books).
2. Tell the story of the wish to a teacher and she will write it down, or write the story of your bear's wish on the bottom of the drawing.
3. Think of three ways to help make your bear's wish come true. Draw a symbol for each of your three ideas, or write the list of the three ideas.
4. Using paper, cloth, cardboard tubes and boxes, and other materials, make something that will help your bear to make his or her wish come true.
5. By now, some bears can probably guess your bear's wishes by what you have made for him. You can each have a turn to share your bear's wish or to ask other children's bears to guess what they think your bear wished for. I'll write down your name, your bear's name, and your bear's wish while you are talking. When everyone has had a turn, we'll look at all the

wishes. We'll see if some bears wished for the same things that other bears wished for, or if some children wished for the same things that their bears wished for!

UNDERSTANDING FRIENDSHIP

Objective: To help children explore peer issues within the classroom setting. To help children integrate a new class member.

Strategy: Focus children on the issue of the bears' relationships with one another.

Book to read at bear meeting: Chester's Way, by Kevin Henkes.

Post read-aloud conversation topics (these topics may be brought up at more than one meeting): What did you think about *Chester's Way*? Does it remind you of anything? What happens when a new kid comes to our classroom? What happens in our classroom when two friends are playing together and then a third kid comes along and wants to play too? How does it feel when kids say, "I'm not your friend"? What do kids mean when they say that? Why do you think it's hard for kids in (pre-K, kindergarten, or 1st grade) to have more than one friend at one time? How do friendships work? Can friends feel angry at each other and stay friends? Can friends want to play alone or with other kids sometimes? Why do you think so? Even though kids don't always feel like playing together, or they get angry at one another, or might have a hard time playing with more than one kid, how can we make sure that all the kids in our classroom community feel likable and valuable (know that we care about them)? What happens when our bears play together? Do they have troubles in their friendships sometimes? Tell us some things that have happened when your bears have played together. What happens if one bear tells another bear that he's not her friend? How can we help them so they feel good and lovable even if another bear doesn't want to play with them at that moment?

Activities that support exploration of topic:

1. Write the children's verbal contributions after the story. Keep their written thoughts handy on an easel where it is easily accessible and can be referred to.
2. Encourage children to do puppet shows about classroom dynamics. (How are the dynamics now and how would they like them to be?)
3. Have kids make paper-doll representations of their bears. Label each bear with its name and laminate it. Attach the paper-doll bears to a board with Velcro dots. Make them available to kids who want to "tell a story" about things that happen with their bear and their bear's friends. Children who engage in this activity may also like to make a representation of themselves and their peers and may want to play to clarify a dynamic that has already happened by acting it out with the dolls.
4. Choose books that reflect the issues that children have brought up during the post-read-aloud session and in the classroom. Read them at bear circle and have them available for children to read on their own.
5. Refer back to the themes, strategies, ideas, and feelings that have come up throughout the study of bear friendships, when applicable, to reframe difficult peer dynamics between children and offer them the option of using some of the strategies they designed for the bears.

A STORY OF EMERGENT CURRICULUM: THE WEDDING

Ms. L's kindergarten class had been using bears for some months working on the above themes when Aaron and Kyle, two little boys, approached her with their bears in hand.

"Our bears want to get married," they announced.

Ms. L was interested in helping the children explore this idea, since fantasies about romance and marriage are common in the kindergarten classroom.

"Why do they want to get married?" Ms. L. inquired.

"Because they are best friends," the boys answered.

"O.K.," Ms. L agreed. "If they get married, what will that mean?"

"It means they stay in the same house forever, silly," Kyle answered.

"Kyle, don't you want to take Cocoa home to your house and not to Aaron's house?" questioned Michael, another boy. "Because Ms. L said we can take our bears home when school's finished.

The boys thought for a minute. "They could trade houses, maybe," offered Aaron. "Or they can be married in school and get divorced when school is done." Kyle nodded in agreement.

"What do they need to do in order to get married? asked Ms. L. "How would you like to help them?"

The boys thought about this. "They have to have a bride and groom," said Aaron.

"O.K. Who is the bride and who is the groom?" The boys looked at each other. They had both assumed that their bears, Cocoa and Fluffy, were boys.

"Can they both be boys for a bride and groom?" wondered Kyle aloud.

"Yes," answered a little girl playing nearby. "Because my two dads had a wedding when they got married."

"No," another girl insisted. "If you have a bride, the bride has to be a girl!"

"You can decide about what Cocoa and Fluffy want to be in this wedding, because it is your idea," offered Ms. L.

The boys talked it over. They decided that Fluffy would be the girl and thus be the bride, and Cocoa would be the boy and the groom.

"Fluffy can be the girl bear because my mom is good at making fancy dresses. When you get married the bride has to wear fancy dresses," Aaron said.

"Well, it takes a long time to plan a wedding," said Ms. L. "Let's study about weddings for a while, and that will help us plan Cocoa and Fluffy's wedding. What does the rest of the class know about weddings? Let's ask the kids at meeting time."

When meeting time came, Aaron and Kyle had a chance to ask their peers what they knew about weddings. Ms. L. wrote their answers down on easel paper.

"You say 'I do,'" Michael said.

"You hold hands and kiss the bride," Rhonda added.

"You have a big giant cake to eat!" Andrew said, jumping up from his seat.

"You have to send out the invitations first of all. That's what my Auntie Rochelle did," added Jayla.

"You really know a lot about weddings," Ms. L commented. "It sounds like we have a lot to do."

"Aaron and me will make the invitations, since our bears are the ones getting married," Kyle said proudly.

"Who would Cocoa and Fluffy like to invite to their wedding?" Ms. L wondered. "Will they invite the other bears, or the children, or both?"

"Just their best friends," said Aaron.

The other kids were silent for a moment.

"I wonder how the other bears would feel about that?" asked Ms. L.

"Bad. They would feel bad and left out," answered Kiara.

"We have to think about what the other bears and the other children could do so that everyone can be part of the celebration," Ms. L told the children.

"My bear only wants his friends to come," repeated Aaron.

"Well, my bear wants her friends to come," added Kyle.

"You know, in a lot of weddings, the groom's family and friends sit on one side and the bride's family and friends sit on the other side," said Ms. L. "Kyle can make a list of bears for Fluffy to invite, and Aaron can make a list of bears for Cocoa to invite. All the children and bears need to be included by the bride or the groom, so you two will need to make sure that your lists cover all the children and bears."

"Yeah, Aaron. If Fluffy doesn't like someone, they can sit on Cocoa's side," Kyle said.

"O.K.," agreed Aaron.

"Your best friend can be your best man," added Jayla.

"But Kyle is my best friend. That's why Fluffy and Cocoa are best friends, and that's why they're getting married," Aaron explained.

"Oh," said Jayla.

"There's just one more thing," said Kyle. "And that is the invitations."

"Jayla, do you still have the invitation that your auntie sent you? Bring it in and let Aaron and Kyle look at it so they can see what a wedding invitation is like. Who would like to think about finding a recipe for a cake that we could make?" Ms. L said.

"Me! Me!" answered Rhonda and Andrew.

Chrystal raised her hand. "Ms L? We forgot about the presents! If you go to a wedding, you gotta bring a present."

There was some disagreement about that point. "No! That's for a birthday party!" a group of children protested.

"My auntie got lots of presents when she got married!" Jayla said seriously.

"Well, if you and your bears are going to make presents for Fluffy and Cocoa, we will have to find out what they like and what they need. Who would like to be in charge of talking to Fluffy and Cocoa about what they want? You can make a list for the class to read at meeting. You can write the words down, or you can draw a picture of the present, or you can do both. Aaron and Kyle will have to look at the calendar and choose a date for the wedding. We need a couple of weeks to plan the wedding and get things ready, so choose a date that comes in February. It's January fifteenth right now, so how many days until February comes?" Ms. L pointed to the classroom calendar as she spoke. The kids counted.

"Nineteen!!!" yelled the children.

"I got a great idea!" said Tyler. "They can get married on Valentine's Day!"

"Yeah! Yeah!" other kids chimed in.

"But that's too far away!" Kyle protested.

"But Kyle," said Aaron patiently. "Don't you want Cocoa and Fluffy to get nice presents? We have to have a lot of days to make their presents and bake the cake!"

Kyle considered those factors. "O.K.," he agreed. The kids cheered.

THE GIFTS OF EMERGENT CURRICULUM

The wedding of Cocoa and Fluffy gave the children in Ms. L's class an opportunity to study a subject that was compelling to them as 5 and 6 year olds who are interested in participating in the kinds of relationships and rituals in which they see adults participating. Fluffy and Cocoa's wedding let the kids explore and pretend about an adult ritual and also gave them a number of problems to solve. What does a wedding involve? What does it mean? How is it done? How will everyone be included? The children had to make lists and represent ideas for gifts. They had to work with the calendar to plan a date; find recipes; and measure, pour, and combine the correct amount of ingredients. They wrote invitations in a particular style. Along with having the opportunity to master these cognitive challenges, the children listened to one another's comments and learned about different kinds of families and ways in which different cultures celebrate marriage. This rich curriculum culminated in a wedding ceremony that was attended by all of the Teddy Bears and all of the children, as well as the children's parents.

CHAPTER 7

Bears in 1st, 2nd, and 3rd Grades: Working with Meaningful Common Ground Themes

HAVING TEDDY BEARS in 1st-, 2nd-, and 3rd-grade classrooms can offer teachers and children a way of making abstract curricular themes come to life so that they can become more meaningful for young learners. At this age, children are starting to be less egocentric and more adept at considering things that are out of the particular current moment of their own personal experience. Thinking about past and future goes beyond what happened yesterday or what will happen tomorrow. Children in the early grades often work on making personal and historical time lines. They are taught to tell time using analog as well as digital clocks to facilitate understanding of what time is all about. They become fascinated with stories about how things were "in the old days," when their own parents and grandparents were children. Because time is an abstract concept, it is introduced in multiple subject areas, including math, social studies, and literacy.

Children in the early grades who are well cared for in the present may have an easier time departing from the present moment to look either at the past or fantasize or predict about the future. Children who experience a lot of stress in the present may have more difficulty developing the perspective necessary to grasp the abstract concepts of past and future times, and may have difficulty integrating past experience with present circumstances.

The following sample activities illustrate the ways in which teachers can use Teddy Bears to help early-grade children develop their knowledge of time.

TEDDY'S WORLD OF TODAY

Objective: To help children develop their awareness of the world around them as a precursor for considering past and future perspectives. To introduce concepts that create a foundation for the understanding of life experience within a historical context.

Strategy: To focus children on the characteristics of their immediate environment, inside and outside the classroom, using bears to give them a new lens for viewing the familiar. To focus children on the ways in which people interact with one another in the world of the here and now that they are sharing with their Teddy Bears.

Books to read for read-aloud: *Ellen Fremedon: Journalist,* by Joan Givner; *Ernie and the Big Newz: The Adventures of a T.V. Reporter*, by Ernie Anastos.

Post read-aloud conversation topics: What did you think about that story? Did it remind you of anything? How do you think it would be to report the news on TV (or in a newspaper) like Ellen and Ernie did? What do you think they had to learn to do to be good reporters? What did you learn about Ernie and Ellen's worlds from their reports? Is this story about a kid who lived a long time ago or a kid who lives in our time? How can you tell? How would you explain ways to tell a "long-ago" story from a "here-and-now" story to your Teddy Bear?

Activities to support exploration of theme:

1. Children take turns using clipboards to record (through writing and drawing) the important features and events that are happening in the classroom during

a 10-minute period in the afternoon. They need to share their report with their Teddy Bear. Once all of the children have had a chance to do this, each child reads his report to all of the bears who are assembled on the rug or in a circle of chairs.

2. *Group discussion*: What did the Teddy Bears learn about life in our classroom during afternoon time?

3. Teddy Bears get a turn to study the world that they can see from the window for a 10-minute period during the afternoon time, and children help them record their observations of important features or events on the clipboard.

4. Teddy Bears share their observations with the whole group.

5. What did the bears learn about life in the world outside the building in the afternoon? Bears share their observations with the whole group.

6. *Discussion*: Did the bears mostly notice the same things or did each one notice different things? What made those things meaningful to the bears?

7. Have the children describe and represent the world that they and their bears are living in right now on a classroom collage or mural. They can write like a reporter, draw, use glue and construction paper or magazine cutouts to create imagery, or write a poem on what they and their bears learned about observing the here and now. (In 3rd grade, information can be gathered from other sources as well—i.e., school and community newspapers.) The teacher will mark the month, day, and year at the top of the mural.

IMAGINING TEDDY'S PAST

Objective: To encourage children to think about what came before their present experience. To foster children's ability to think sequentially, appreciate cause-and-effect relationships, and connect to the process of their own growth and evolution.

Strategy: To focus children on creating a history for their Teddy Bears that elaborates their life story before they came into the school setting. To help children investigate their own past experiences by using photographs and interviewing adults who knew them when they were younger.

Books for read-aloud: *When I Was Little,* by Jamie Lee Curtis; *When Grandpa Was Young,* by Heather Hammonds

Post read-aloud discussion topics: What did you think about that book? Did it remind you of anything? What do you think happened in your Teddy Bear's life before he came to live at our school? What are some ways of knowing what happened before the time that is now? Remind us how old your Teddy Bear is. If your Teddy is very young, will he have a long story of his life before he came to our school, or a short story? If your Teddy is a teenager or a grown-up, will she have a longer story or a shorter story? Why?

Activities that support exploration of topics:

1. Ask the children to write and illustrate the story of their Teddy Bears' lives, beginning when they were made and ending when they came to live in the classroom. What were the experiences and adventures that their Teddies had after being made and before coming here? (Second and 3rd graders can write multichapter stories.)

2. Ask the children to think of the important things that have happened in their lives between when they were born and when they came to (1st, 2nd, or 3rd) grade. They can make an index card for each year of their lives and draw a picture of something that happened at that time. Then, the kids can make a time line with their index cards by putting them in order on a long piece of paper. (First graders can write captions for the cards. Second and 3rd graders can write at greater length about the times they chose to illustrate.)

3. Invite parents to come in and tell stories about how things were when they were little. Encourage them to bring artifacts. Children and their bears listen to the stories together. They can ask questions about life in the times that are being described. Did the parents have Teddies when they were children? Is there a story about their Teddies?

4. Also invite grandparents to come in and tell stories about how things were when they were little. Ask them to bring artifacts. Children and their bears will listen to the stories together. They can ask questions about the times that are being described. Did the grandparents have Teddies when they were little? Is there a story associated with it?

5. Hold a group discussion in morning meeting. Discuss: What things about being a kid in school have changed over time? What things have stayed the same? The teacher will record the responses on easel paper.

6. Do a class project about times past. The kids can read "Once Upon a Time" books about how things were and how they changed over time; write memory books, do small-group skits or a class play, and so an. Projects should capture sequence and process.

TEDDY IN THE FUTURE

Objective: To encourage children to conceptualize, fantasize, think about, and plan for time beyond the here and now.

Strategy: Use Teddy Bears as a nonthreatening way to play with the idea of creating dreams and plans for the future.

Books for read-aloud: *Nicky the Jazz Cat*, by Carol Friedman; *Appelemondo's Dream*, by Patricia Polanco; *The Time Warp Trio, 2095*, by Jon Scieszka.

Post read-aloud discussion topics: What did you and your bear think about that book? Did it remind you of anything? Do you think our school will be the same as it is now in the future or do you think it will be different? Do you think new things will be invented that haven't been invented yet? What do you think your Teddy will do when he is older? What would he like his world to be like in the future? What do you think he would like to do in the future? How can he get ready to do that little by little? Do you think your Teddy would like to change something about the world when he is older? What would it be?

Activities to support exploration of topic:

1. Ask the children to write and illustrate a story about what their Teddy Bears would like to do in the world when they are all grown up.
2. Have the children write and illustrate a story about what they would like to do when they are grown up.
3. The children can make a collection of things and symbols of things that they think would help them and their Teddies to achieve their goals.
4. Together with their Teddies, children can invent something new that kids in the future might like to use. They can use boxes, cardboard tubes and cylinders, wood pieces, and other materials that they find among the class's construction and collage material. They could paint or color their invention. They and their "bear partner" will have a turn to introduce their invention to the class and tell everyone what it will do to make life better in the world of the future.
5. Children can draw out (or write out) the process of how they built their invention and how their invention will work. Invite parents into the classroom to see and learn about the children's inventions for the future.

THE STORY OF AN EMERGENT THEME:
HURTING AND HEALING

The themes of hurting and healing often appeal to very young children who are trying to resolve body-integrity issues as they play. Preschool children frequently pretend to be doctors to care for sick stuffed animals or baby dolls. When Teddy Bears are present in 1st, 2nd, and 3rd grade, as well as pre-K and kindergarten, hurting and healing themes often emerge as the children interact with their bears (see Plate 6). These themes are sometimes explored collaboratively in pretend play about taking the bears to the vet, or result in studies that explore the role of the vet in the community. More often, these themes are explored individually as children use their bears to help them integrate their own experiences with hurting and healing.

Hurting and healing themes are often motivating to 1st- through 3rd-grade children who have some unresolved concerns about physical well-being, psychological hurts that are hard to heal, or ongoing medical issues. The presence of Teddy Bears, Band-Aids, and creative materials that can be used to craft medical equipment can be a powerful invitation to children who need to make their own medical experiences less overwhelming, or symbolize invisible hurts. In addition, children may make their bears represent injuries that happen to peers that they find unsettling. Some of the bears pictured in Plate 6 became "injured" after one classmate broke his foot.

> "My bear Samantha just got her tonsils out. She can't eat
>   anything but Jell-O and ice cream."
> "Koala fell down from the tree and sprained her ankle, so
>   now she has to wear this bandage. I have to carry her
>   all day."
> "This is the emergency room. The yellow cup is the oxygen
>   mask. I have to hold him while they give him the
>   oxygen, because he's scared when they put that over
>   his face."

The child who silently puts many Band-Aids on her bear may be involved in an activity that helps her to heal the hurts that distract her during the literacy block, or compel her to act aggressively with another child on the playground. The teacher who invites children to identify with the hurt Teddy Bear as well as with the healer gives children a representational voice for their body-integrity issues, and may help to alleviate the preoccupation with these issues. Teachers can invite children to extend their interest in this theme by writing about both their Teddies' and their own experiences with hurt and healing. This can take the form of journal writing, story writing, and story acting, as well as song writing and poetry.

One of the comments heard most often from teachers who use Teddy Bears in the classroom is that the bears help the children to be more empathetic to others and ultimately promote pro-social behavior. This developmental milestone happens when the Teddy Bear project is done by an empathetic teacher who can help children become more empathetic to their own injuries and losses. The Teddy is often the first recipient of the child's empathetic response, and the other children come next. Allowing emergent themes of hurting and healing to flourish within the classroom helps it to become a more caring environment.

CHAPTER 8

The Story of Bears in the Upper Grades

MOST UPPER-GRADE TEACHERS would have a hard time conceiving of accommodating Teddy Bears in their academically driven classrooms. However, creative teachers may want to integrate this practice into upper-school grades so that the students have the opportunity to use a transitional object in a new and more sophisticated way. Indeed, children in their final year of elementary school often worry about the transition to the larger world of middle school and are distracted by this worry at intervals during the school year. Introducing bears in the second half of the school year as a way of facilitating separation may be appealing to upper-grade as well as lower-grade teachers (see Chapter 10: "Bears Say Good-Bye"). This may be a powerful intervention for groups of children who have had a lot of loss prior to the separation from their elementary school teachers and peers.

Ms. Y started out as one of several substitute teachers who came to teach in the 5th-grade class at Miller Elementary School after the classroom teacher became ill in late October. The children gave Ms. Y a hard time, as most children do when there is a substitute teacher in the classroom. They were attached to their original teacher and wanted her back. Unfortunately, their teacher was then diagnosed with a serious heart ailment that would require surgery and a long recovery period. Her doctors advised her to stay out of school for the rest of the school year. When this was finally determined and communicated to the children, they became even more enraged and uncooperative. Having to separate from their beloved teacher in this unanticipated way while they prepared to leave their school and go to middle school evoked too much loss for this particular group to handle. This group of smart, active students seemed to be using all of its energy to fight their new teacher's attempts to teach them. Ms. Y began using all of her energy to maintain order and cover curriculum despite the kids' challenging behavior. The use of Teddy Bears in the lower-grade classrooms was part of the usual practice of the Miller School, and Ms. Y decided that all of the children who'd had bears in the lower grades needed to bring them back into the classroom for the rest of the school year. She gave new bears to children who had transferred into the school or had not kept their early-grade Teddies.

The group went through the initial process of going back to identify their bears and communicate about their personalities on a new level. Some identities had changed over the years. Others had remained constant. As the children became reacquainted with their bears and with one another's bears, Ms. Y began to feel more hopeful about the group. She noted that the level of anger and anxiety in the classroom receded when the children were interacting with their bears.

As time went on and the novelty of having the bears back in the classroom began to wear off, Ms. Y felt unsure about where to go with the bears. There was so much material that the class had yet to cover due to all the disruptions in their school year to date. When she tried to focus the class on these academic goals, their difficult behavior increased. She began to look at the 5th-grade curriculum content guide to search for curriculum that might allow for the integrated use of the Teddy Bears. She thought about the possibility of integrating bears into the 5th-grade social studies curriculum. The focus of this curriculum was colonization. Ms. Y did not have to go beyond the introduction of the topic before the kids solved the problem of how to include bears in the study. "Let's make a bear colony!" they suggested. After many group conversations with the children that focused on generating ideas for addressing 5th-grade social studies, science, and literacy goals through the designing of a bear colony, the plan for Beartown was born.

A TOWN AND ITS INHABITANTS

The colonization curriculum required children to read about the way that the American colonies had become established. The children now sought to apply this learning to the ambitious project of starting a colony for their bears. They petitioned the school principal for permission to establish a colony and for space within the school to do so. They developed a charter for the bear colony based on the charters they read about in their research. They decided on businesses and services that would be necessary for the colonists, and built and advertised these to the residents of the colony. They voted on what to call the colony once it was established. Creating Beartown became a rich and elaborate curricular project that required children to read, write, problem-solve, budget, and make use of historical context and historical perspective (see Figures 8.1 and 8.2).

The inhabitants of Beartown were both precious and very familiar to the children. That allowed the Beartown project to go beyond the learning that supported the establishment of a mock colony, and include the exploration of interpersonal issues and quality-of-life experiences of the town's residents: namely, the Teddy Bears. Children invented a Beartown newspaper, a Beartown CD with songs written by the bears and their owners, and a post office for Teddy Bear letters, allowing the bears many vehicles for self-expression within their community. As voices for the bears, the children were able to address and explore complex relationship issues that 11 year olds are beginning to sort out. Preadolescent themes about marriage, divorce, reconciliation, love, loss, and death were present in the older children's writing. The children's freedom to integrate life-experience issues into their literacy and social studies curriculum made this curriculum especially compelling for them, which showed up in the high quality of the children's work (see Figure 8.3).

Beartown became a place of interest within the Miller School community. Other children were curious about Beartown and wanted to know what it was all about. Ms. Y's 5th graders decided

FIGURE 8.1. Fifth graders used their bears to make their study of colonization come alive.

To the queen's most excellent Majesty,

The colonists of Beartown and I have come up with an idea that we may be able to bring Beartown into the future with help from you. We may even get to a point where we can have electricity in our homes and buildings. To make this work, we will need cardboard to make houses, signs, and other building markers to draw and write things on the signs and maby plastic to put on windows of houses.

Some of the buildings we will/might have in our village/colony are maby a library, post office, town hall, and a couple of farms.

We will go about doing this as bears by working our hardest and if we get stuck, we'll ask our human friends for help. But even though we're bears doesn't mean that we can't do some of it ourselves.

We will regularly inform you of our programs by sending down two bears that we will elect in town hall. And each week they could inform you of all progress like plants and crop growth, economie progress. And progress of colony growth.

You can expect crops and food like corn, carrots, peppers, and po-tatoes and goods like animal skins, gold, and other things. And you can expect loyal subjects for this generous donation of land and loyalty. I as an individual can't really say how we can go about doing things to meet the standards but I know we will try our best to please you.

Sinserly,
B. Wellington III (David C.'s Bear)

---

to make Beartown open to the public at certain days and times. They invited other classrooms of children to come and visit, and to bring their Teddy Bears along in case they wanted to visit with other bears or to buy needed items in Beartown's stores. The children of the Miller School's lower grades were enthralled. They loved coming to Beartown and shopping for their bears. The 5th graders felt admired and appreciated. Their sense of efficacy, competence, and value grew as Beartown grew more and more important within the school (see Appendix A).

FIGURE 8.2. "The history of Beartown, the story of a colony"
by Annique

CHAPTER 1: BEARTOWN BEARS

Beartown bears are cute, little stuffed animals. Namely, Teddy Bears! They are all golden-brown, with the exception of a bear named Ivy, who is the color of white sand. They all live in a place called 'Beartown' which is lovated in the Jackson Street School Courtyard. There, they live in houses, that they built, and run businesses that they founded. They all moved out of Ms. Y's Classroom when the colony could no longer fit! They were nt alone in this move, though. A young bear from the sunset grizzly tribe (more on the tribes later), named Shimma Cr'Ball, and her apprentice, Artemis Jaguarondi, came with them. Now, Shimma was a bear, alright. Blended right in. Same color fur and everything. But she still has the beliefs of a sunset grizzly, trust us. Recently, Shimma's apprentice, Artemis, opened a library. A nice, quiet place where a bear can go to relax after a long, hard day. Shimma, on the other hand, is much more outgoing. She opened a spa/gift shop. Pathetic.

CHAPTER 2: THE SUNSET GRIZZLEY TRIBE

The sunset grizzly tribe is a rowdy tribe that likes going all-out in the world. And yet, they live in hiding. Their secret places? Why, the nooks and crannies of the school's upper floors! While you'll certainly never see one for very long, if you're lucky, you may see one dash across the hall, or one of their apprentices, who are almost always snow leopard cubs (more on that later), reading, out of the corner of your eye. If your lucky. They are very tricky and quick though. So when you look closer, they probably won't be there.

CHAPTER 3: THE BLACK CREEK TRIBE

Scarcely ever seen, the black creek tribe is the exact opposite of the sunset grizzly tribe. Where the grizzlies are golden-brown, the black creeks are black. Where the grizzlies are out-going, the blacks are shy. Where the grizzlies are ruthless, the blacks are sweet. Where most grizzlies areen't very smart, and honor a smart person (like Shimma) as a miracle, the blacks are extremely smart. See why they're at war? They each have different tactics. This usually makes the cubs support the blacks. A sighting of a black creek bear is very very very very very rare, and should be reported at once! It will make the news!

CHAPTER 4: SNOW LEOPARDS, AND HOW THEY FIT INTO THIS

The snow leopards were saved by the grizzlies a long time ago, and, while many favor the black creek tribe for being so peaceful, and clever, they still have to pay off their ancestors debt.

Figure 8.3. Songs, newsletters, and other creative forms of expression captured the 5th graders' need to make sense of relationships.

Figure 8.3a. Songs—"The Cinderbears Presents: New Beginnings"

WHY CAN'T WE BE DUCKS?

Everyday, everyone tellin' us what to do—and I get sick of it, yeah, its true. I just want to be different—if they say that we're bears is that really true? Have you ever seen bears do what me and you do? Chorus: why can't we be ducks, ducks, ducks—if we want to and we're blue—and we're so tired of these dues, why can't we be ducks/and then we'd play all day, and then we'd play—yeah we'd make you say let's all play (first verse again, chorus twice)

NEW BEGINNINGS

Meeting new people happens everyday—and if we could we'd run away—but we can't—if we really care, yeah we'll be there—just hold on—but we won't have any fun-and just watch all the new beginnings. Chorus: why can't we, just stay home?—I just wish, we'd be alone ooooooooohhh-hh! But time is on our side, yeah time is on our side. When we meet new people, sometimes we like them, sometimes we don't—but just watch all the new beginnings. (chorus twice)

BIO OF SINGER/SONGWRITER DUCK DUDEMEISTER (BEAR)

Duck lived in the rainforest deep in the heart of Brazil, until his anger management made him make the decision to move to America, where he could have therapeutic attention. Duck enjoys riding large animals and pretending that he can fly.

Figure 8.3b. "Duck Albanie Dudemeister III"

Duck Dudemeister III was born, 1884 in a remote part of Brazil where he spent most of his childhood swinging from tree to tree. His father, Duck Dudemeister Junior was a well known motivational speaker who came from a long line of Duck Dudemeisters of the same profession. It was quite a shock to his family when Duck III chose a different path.

Delilah Dudemeister was a stay at home mom who left her family when Duck was six. Recently she has come back into contact with him, saying that she never meant for it to happen. Entering adolescence he developed serious anger management problems and was jailed on several occasions because of it. By the time he was jailed for his fifth time, he realized something had to change. At the tender age of 15 he left home and came to Beartown located in Massachusetts.

He signed up for therapy and dedicated himself to becoming more relaxed about his anger. Soon he was greatly improved and in 2003 he started the Cinderbears at age 17. At this time he also met Floppy Snizer his wife to be.

Within two years, Cinderbears were the largest franchise in the country. At this point, Duck started his own line of guitairs and quickly expanded the Cinderbears label to housewear and other such products.

In 2005, Duck was engaged to Floppy Snizer and they were married in Brazil near Duck's hometown, later that year.

Currently, Duck and Floppy are happily married and living with two children, Tzipporah and Duck IIII. They are expecting one more who will be named Georgia. They are living in Beartown MA. Duck continues to write songs with the help of the rest of the Cinderbears and the three of them continue to perform. Floppy works as a banker in downtown Beartown.

Figure 8.3c. "Dudemeister Divorce"

Yesterday afternoon Duck and Floppy made their divorce public. It was quite a surprise to many, as the couple had had a nice marriage for little over 18 years. The couples' relationship had become rocky over the past couple of months, and it was no doubt that Georgia being lost only added to the stress. Duck and Floppy, who has re-attained her first last name of Fong, declined to say a lot, but Duck gave a brief explanation. "I was feeling overworked, Floppy was helping out as much with the family, and Georgia being gone was just making the entire thing worse." Late last night, Duck packed up and moved to long time friend's house, Phil Powinka, and with him went Tzipporah. Duck Dudemeister IIII chose to stay with his mother, and the two are quite pleased with the arrangement. "I think it will be better this way . . . it was great being with Floppy, but if we were meant to be together, I wouldn't be so stressed out all the time. We're still good friends and everything, no hard feelings. I think we both agree this is a better arangement." When asked what impact the divorce would have on his children, Duck III jumped in stoically and said, "I think we will be alright. Anything is better than the fighting."

Ms. Y gave her all to her fifth-grade class, but it was difficult for the children to overcome their sense of loss at losing their old teacher and let Ms. Y take her rightful place in classroom life. Beartown became a place within the classroom where both the children and the new teacher could be comfortable and productive.

WHEN BEARS LOOP

When schools choose to include Teddy Bears in their classrooms at all age levels, teachers may wonder what to do with the bears if they "inherit" bears that have been present at the previous grade level. Certainly, it is important to reintroduce bears to a new class that will usually include new members, and to give bears to those children who do not yet have them because they transferred from another school or lost them over the summer. Some of the initial activities may need to be done again. The beds or houses may not have "looped" with the bears and may need to be redone, this time on another developmental level.

The suggestions for integrating bears into practice that I've given here may help teachers to think about ways they can include bears in existing curriculum, and use them as vehicles for ever-changing developmental, social, and experiential issues that the particular group of children in question brings with them throughout the new school year. As children grow and change, their use of metaphors and symbols becomes more flexible and more complex. Therefore, the upper-grade children whose work is shown in this section are able to create depth of character in their bears and weave their stories about their bears into the social studies curriculum in an inventive and thoughtful way while still deriving comfort and organization from the bears' presence.

When bears loop, the school sends a powerful message about their value in the learning process, as well as sending a message to children about the value of continuity and staying connected to personal history as you grow up.

CHAPTER 9

Bears in Bad Times

THE PREVIOUS CHAPTERS OF this book have described many ways in which comfort objects (or transitional objects) can be growth-promoting for children in the early grades as part of day-to-day practice. When children in the school community experience a loss or trauma, Teddy Bears may be an important facilitator of the healing process. This chapter may be particularly helpful to teachers whose children have experienced an upsetting or traumatic event at school or in the course of the school year.

Teachers often have difficulty knowing how to bring up or address a difficult experience with children. Even in the case of a community trauma, when the traumatic experience has affected everyone, school communities often shy away from acknowledging it within the school environment. Many teachers in New York City during and after September 11, 2001, report being told not to say anything about what happened unless the children brought it up themselves. This advice sounded reassuring to teachers who also felt overwhelmed with fear and loss as a result of the attacks. Unfortunately, for young children who may not be able to organize their thoughts or communicate their perceptions of the events surrounding them, adult silence often results in children becoming isolated with and preoccupied by the traumatic experience. When the "elephant in the room" is allowed to take up emotional space, learning and emotional well-being suffer.

BEARS, BEARS EVERYWHERE

When disastrous events have befallen our country, such as the attacks of September 11, Hurricane Katrina, and the wildfires in

California, relief agencies often distribute Teddy Bears to affected children. Mercy Corps, an international organization that assists children in traumatic times, gives each child a kit that has materials that are designed to provide comfort and invite self-expression. The bear is almost always the first thing that children pull out of the box. After September 11, Teddy Bears flooded the New York City public schools, sent from organizations all over the world to help the children know that they were not alone. (See *Creating Schools That Heal*, Koplow, 2002.)

Indeed, when Teddy Bears are given to children in bad times, it is helpful for the children to know where they came from and why they were given to them. The classroom teacher may use a morning meeting to introduce the bears within the context of the community trauma. For example, she may say, "You know, what happened to us during the [traumatic event] was so scary. People all over the country were thinking about the children who live in our town and how to help them to feel safer. They decided to send us these bears." If the school or the classroom teacher herself is the provider, she may say, "I was thinking about what happened to us, and how scary it was, and I was thinking about ways to help the kids to feel safer. I decided to bring Teddy Bears into the room. Maybe they will help us to feel safer, and maybe we can figure out ways to help them feel safe in our school." This way of introducing the bears both acknowledges the traumatic event and provides a containing response to it.

Children need to have time and space to respond to the topic that has been introduced. They will often take that opportunity to ask questions or make comments about what happened. The teacher may want to hand out the bears while the children are talking, so that they can hold their bears as the difficult material is being articulated. Even the teacher may feel like holding a bear as children express themselves on a traumatic subject!

It is important for the children to say what they need to say without the teacher contradicting the child's feeling about what happened. For example, a young Katrina-affected child who says, "Nobody helped us for so many hours and I was hungry on the roof and I was hot" needs an empathic response such as, "That must have been so hard," rather than an attempt to paint a rosier picture. The teacher may be tempted to say something like, "We tried our hardest to make sure everyone got the help they needed," which in the case of Katrina victims was not the truth and does not reflect the child's experience. After some children have a chance to comment on what happened, the teacher may want to ask the children if they think their bears ever had something really scary happen to them. There will probably be a variety of responses. It is an important invitation, because if children have a traumatic history prior to the community trauma, they are at higher risk for developing Post-Traumatic Stress Disorder (PTSD) and will likely have more difficulty adjusting in the months to follow.

The teacher will want to make sure that there are many invitations for children to symbolize their difficult experiences in a variety of ways. She may make blank books for them to draw in and write in when they are thinking about what happened. She may invite them to use art and building materials to interpret events as they saw them. Introducing the idea that "some of the bears" might remember other scary times may help children create a bridge between past and present to make the prior traumas less isolated or less overwhelming.

When there is a community trauma, the helping professions organize around supporting the survivors. Organizations are more likely to attain public funding for providing outreach, referral services, counseling, and mental health consultation services in the aftermath of the crisis. However, when young children suffer the more private traumas of abuse, neglect, domestic violence, and community violence in their families or in their communities, there is little in place to acknowledge or respond to the overwhelming nature of their life experiences.

A child who acts out his private pain in school will be more likely to be referred for help, but may not be likely to receive help for the trauma he is acting out. Instead, interventions may be organized around eliminating the difficult behavior without addressing its origin. Children who don't act out their pain are no less affected.

The debilitating effects of their traumatic experiences may result in inattention, memory deficits, depression, and emotional isolation at school. At the very least, providing bears for a group of children that includes those kids who are at greater risk due to a traumatic history acknowledges every child's right to be comforted, and gives children permission to acknowledge the hurt that they carry (see Figure 9.1).

REACHING IN/REACHING OUT

Using bears in bad times can help the teacher to reach children who may otherwise have remained emotionally isolated and can encourage children who have been affected by a tragic experience to reach out to others who have also been affected by something difficult and overwhelming. When children who had been affected by the 1994 Oklahoma City bombing sent Teddy Bears with personal notes attached to New York City children after 9/11, 2nd-grade through upper-grade teachers encouraged children to write back to the kids who had sent the bears and develop a pen-pal relationship. This therapeutic assignment connected New York City children to

FIGURE 9.1. "My bear Jack wants to stop war!!"

My bear Jack wants to stop war!!!
Here are three reasons why one: The bombs
wreck our breath taking views. Two: It
kills innocent people like children, women
and men. Three: It destroys everything!!!! Sometimes
he goes to class rooms and talks about why
war is dangerous. Sometimes he needs a student to
help him act so the students can see why
war is dangerous. He also goes to meetings
and talks to people and bears. Jack still
fights with his words for man and bear
kind. By Andrew

same-grade children in another state who knew something about the kind of trauma and loss of security that they were experiencing. A similar school-based intervention helped the child victims of Hurricane Rita to reach out to the children affected by Hurricane Katrina.

When schools use Teddy Bears in lower-grade classrooms as part of emotionally responsive practice, they have a foundation in place for addressing difficult experiences if they happen. The Teddy Bear project is in essence about facilitating a feeling of connection and well-being in children. It is based on heightening child-adult attachment relationships, symbolizing these relationships, and then inviting children to expand their capacity to symbolize, communicate about, and connect to others around their own emotional and actual experiences. When teachers practice an emotionally supportive, pro-social method such as this one, the classroom community has more capacity to function as a holding environment that can contain children through hard times. Receiving and providing comfort are familiar behaviors to students whose primary-school classrooms use bears. Having received empathy on a daily basis within the classroom environment, children develop a basis for self-comfort as well as for extending empathy to others in need.

Every classroom will have some children who have experienced loss and other disturbing events prior to the community tragedy, while others have not. All children in the classroom will react to bad times within the context of their prior life experiences, which will be somewhere on a continuum from manageable to profoundly disorganizing. One child's emotional pain may connect to the death of a parent, while another child's emotional distress may be evocative of a lost pet or a missed school bus. Most children regress during highly stressful or tragic times. The classroom that acknowledges that people have both good and bad times and provides empathy to children when times are bad models a compassionate response to emotional pain and universalizes children's need to sometimes express negative affects.

CHAPTER 10

Bears Say Good-Bye

SAYING GOOD-BYE IS NOT easy for young children, especially if the good-byes in their lives have been abrupt or traumatic. It isn't easy for many teachers, either. Separation can make teachers recall prior separations and losses that they may feel they need distance from. As a teacher gets ready to separate from the children who have been in her classroom and in her thoughts, and sometimes even in her dreams for an entire school year, she may find herself feeling an array of powerful emotions that may be uncomfortable. These may include loss, relief, pride, guilt, concern, sadness, joy, and sometimes a sense of emotional exhaustion. She may be uncertain about the value of expressing these feelings while she is with the children and may instead feel she needs to be more detached as the last day of school draws near.

Given the unresolved developmental issues that separation may evoke in children and the unresolved life-experience issues that separation may evoke in parents, children, and teachers, the end of the school year can be an emotionally tumultuous time.

Children and adults tend to express separation anxiety very differently from one another. Children who become anxious about leaving their teachers, classmates, and classroom may seem to be regressing in school. They may seem to have "forgotten" the social rules that have been in place for a long time. They may act less respectful of the teacher's authority, voice disdain for their classroom environment, or express enthusiasm and impatience for moving on to the next level. Teachers may feel that certain children are psychologically absent long before the last day of school comes around. Teachers may feel, to some degree, that they've been defeated and abandoned by these students for whom they worked so hard.

In addition to their own separation reactions, teachers often feel very stressed at the end of the school year by administrative demands that require them to remove attention from interpersonal issues and focus on paperwork, housekeeping, and other organizational tasks. Children often react to the subtle but powerful shift in their teacher's attentions by feeling abandoned and resentful and acting out in ways that demand that she shift her attention back to them. Children who have a history of disrupted attachment relationships or prior traumatic losses are especially vulnerable to regression at the end of the school year, as separation from their teacher, classmates, and school routines evokes their earlier experiences. Even when teachers manage to stay present with their students through the last day of school, young children may feel rejected by not being "allowed to" return to their classroom teacher in the fall. Young children may imagine that teachers have the power to "keep them" if they really wanted to, or perhaps go along with them to the next grade. They may experience hurt and disappointment when they find out that this will not happen. Parents may express their own separation anxiety by talking about the next teacher or classroom in glowing terms, and referring to what a "big kid" their child is getting to be; but these words may not feel reassuring to the young child who may not feel ready to leave a secure and familiar classroom environment behind.

BEARS GET READY: THE TRANSITION OUT

While many schools organize end-of-year parties or performances, these events tend not to help children process the experience of separating. Parties are usually associated with birthdays in the minds of children. Performances often require hours of practicing and perfecting song-and-dance routines that may be much appreciated by parents but distract children and teachers from saying good-bye to one another and to the classroom experience that they created and shared. It is important for teachers and school administrators to invent curriculum and rituals that are meaningful to the children as part of the separation process.

When classrooms have used Teddy Bears as part of their practice, the bears can be a helpful bridge for the children who are in the process of making the big transition from one school year to the next. Bears go home with children at the end of the school year. When schools use bears in all primary-grade classrooms, they often advance to the next level with the children. The bears' role as transitional objects offers children a feeling of continuity through a period of change and allows them the possibility of separating while still remaining emotionally connected to their teachers who provided the bears, and to their own emotional experience as they say good-bye.

The timing of facilitating the separation process can be difficult. Children need to be able to anticipate the cycle of the school year and need to have information about when it will be over. When the dialogue is initiated too early in the school year, young children who have little understanding of time may mistakenly conclude that the separation is imminent. On the other hand, when teachers wait until the last week of school to address the separation, children have very little time to process this within the classroom. Most of the time it works to initiate the dialogue in May or early June (4 to 6 weeks before the end of the school year) so that children have time to process the upcoming transition with their teacher and classmates in a containable way.

Teachers may want to introduce the topic of transition in a morning meeting with children and bears present. She may direct the children's attention to the calendar, and focus on the number of days or weeks until the last day of school. She writes "last day of school" on the day that marks the end of the school year. Then she may go back to the page of the calendar that refers to the previous September, where the first day of school was marked. The kids might want to count all of the days or weeks that they have been together.

The teacher might say, "We have been together for many days and weeks and months. We've really gotten to know one another well. You have learned so many new things and we have done so many interesting things together. Now it's almost time to say good-bye. I wonder how it feels to you and your bears to be almost finished with   [grade level]   ."

Children respond for themselves or for their bears, expressing a variety of thoughts and feelings about the end of the year. Children who have trouble owning sad, fearful, or angry affects may be more inclined to let those feelings be attributed to their bears. This invitation to have a voice for thoughts, feelings, and fantasies about the transition can help to facilitate a more productive separation process for both children and teachers as the children experience their teachers as "being with them" as they talk together and include their transitional objects in the dialogue.

The teacher can encourage the children and bears to think about all that they have done together and experienced together as a group. What were the most amazing times, the saddest times, the scariest times, the happiest times? This kind of collective retrospective focuses the children on the shared experiences that have shaped the classroom culture and community that they have become. It also communicates that their experiences are valuable and meaningful to the teacher as well as to the children. Many activities that support the process can follow these dialogues, such as making a classroom scrapbook, individual good-bye books, and art and writing projects about what children and bears want to take with them to the next grade and what they wish they could leave behind.

An important component of helping children to have a "good good-bye" involves inviting the children to think about and plan for what might help their Teddy Bears "feel ready" to say good-bye to their classroom. Children whose bears do feel ready can be engaged in helping peers whose bears don't feel ready. Children may answer the question in a variety of ways, depending on their grade level and their feelings about the end of the year: "My bear needs to play bingo one more time," "My bear doesn't feel ready because she can't read yet," or "My bear needs to get all the other bears' addresses so she can have pen pals over the summer." All of these responses can invite group brainstorming and planning for helping the bears to feel ready for the transition. The class may schedule another bingo game for the bear who needs one. The child whose bear wants summer pen pals can make a list of her classmates' bears and collect their addresses. The kids can decide to help the nonreader bear to learn to read, or they may find ways to reassure him that he can learn at home or in the next grade. All of these activities encourage the group to remain a group throughout the separation process, and help the children feel that they are in "good company" (see Figure 10.1).

SAYING GOOD-BYE: REAL AND PRETEND

Teachers may have many emotions as the school year draws to a close. One of the emotions is almost always relief. Teaching is an intense experience, and by the end of June, most teachers welcome the summer break as a time to renew themselves and refuel before the next group of kids enters their lives. Most children voice relief and joy about being finished with the end of the school year, but in reality, school may be the only stimulating, dependable, and nurturing environment that some children have. Children who have difficult home lives may feel a loss of protection and care at the end of the school year, and may even feel endangered by it. Often, these ambivalent feelings play out in the classroom during the last weeks of the school year, increasing the teacher's need to provide relief.

It is problematic to paint summer vacation as a gift if it is felt as a loss by members of the classroom community. It is important to acknowledge the reality of the children's experience of vacation as it comes near. Teddy Bears can be useful in helping to facilitate a dialogue around the group's ambivalence about vacation. The teacher can ask children how their bears feel about the idea of living at their houses for the summer and not coming to school. She can ask children to make an entry in their bear's journal about how they think it will be. Kids can be encouraged to make a plan for

Figure 10.1. Children reflect on and represent the ways that their bears have grown and changed during the school year.

their bears so they won't be bored or feel lonely without the other bears around. These may result in children making play dates for their bears, or thinking about bringing them along on a family vacation, or writing a list of all the shows their bears will watch together at the babysitter's house. In any of these scenarios, the teacher is helping the children to build bridges between the life they have had during the school year and the life they have at home during the summertime.

Courtesy of Teddy Bears

WHILE I HAVE USED THE Teddy Bear technique in a variety of settings for many years, the process of writing this book gave me new insights and brought opportunities to talk with teachers about the ways in which the bears affect classroom climate. Many teachers expressed the fact that there was less anxiety and less volatility in the classroom once Teddy Bears became a part of classroom life. Others reported more pro-social behavior as a result of the project and less violence among the children. Some teachers found their children to be more receptive to learning once the bears were involved in literacy and social studies activities.

One interesting outcome of my interviews with teachers and observations in elementary schools that use bears was the realization of how powerful the Teddy Bear Project was for many of the boys. This surprised teachers, who assumed that beyond pre-K and kindergarten, the boys would not be very interested in using Teddy Bears and would protest their involvement. On the contrary, it seemed that boys were particularly empowered by this invitation to create and care for a comfort object. Teachers felt that the boys' interest in the project kept pace with, and at times surpassed, the interest of the girls, and that this was consistent throughout the primary grades.

While girls tend to be given stuffed animals and dolls to play with throughout childhood, boys are more frequently encouraged to interact with these toys only in infancy and toddlerhood. Therefore, they may have had less experience with stuffed animals and less opportunity to explore their use. The Teddy Bear Project implicitly gave boys "permission" to have and interact with a comfort object of their own in an atmosphere where this kind of interaction was the norm. The fact that children of both sexes had bears allowed boys to engage with the bears more deeply and with less conflict, and to reap the benefits of this kind of relationship-based supportive curriculum.

When a group of 3rd graders were interviewed about the benefits of having Teddy Bears in the classroom, one boy raised his hand to comment: "I think having a bear in school is important because it gives you an idea of how it feels to take care of something. Usually you have to wait until you grow up and have kids to do that." This comment articulates the power of the transitional object to function as a link to the future, as well as to the present and the past. For this little boy, as well as for many others, the attachment to his bear and his role as a caregiver helped him to see himself in a positive, nurturing role.

Given the recent rise in concern about boys being at risk in the school environment, this outcome seems important to note (see Plate 7).

Courtesy of Teddy Bears, hundreds of young schoolchildren have found a way to feel safe and connected in school, and that has allowed them to connect to teachers and other children, and to discover their own learning potential in a more positive way. Hopefully, *Bears, Bears Everywhere!* will result in even greater numbers of Teddy Bears coming to school.

Beartown Documents

FIGURE A.1. Grade 5 curriculum.

SCIENCE AND TECHNOLOGY/ENGINEERING

Physical Science

State Standards—Benchmarks

Rocks and Minerals   Earth's Systems
Plants   Animals
Sound   Electricity
Matter   Forces

Student will be able to:

1. Recall basic information about review units.
2. Explain concepts covered in review units.
3. Provide and support evidence to prove concepts covered in review units

Technology/Engineering

State Standards—Benchmarks

Engineering Design

Student will be able to:

1. Identify relevant design features (e.g., size, shape, weight) for building a prototype of a solution to a given problem.
2. Identify the factors that engineers and builders must consider when they design structures.
3. Build a structure using proper tools and materials to solve the above problem.
4. Conduct an evaluation and test of the structure for effectiveness, efficiency, and aesthetics.
5. Describe different ways in which a problem can be represented, e.g., sketches, diagrams, graphic organizers, and lists.
6. Illustrate and explain different ways to represent a given problem.
7. Use at least two techniques to represent a given problem and two techniques to represent possible solutions to that problem.

Figure A.1. Grade 5 curriculum (*continued*).

SOCIAL STUDIES CURRICULUM

Geography
History
Economics
Civics and Government
Maps and Globe Skills
Basic U.S. Physical and Political Geography

Exploration

—European explorers
—Causes and effects

Colonization

—Settlements
—Colonies
—Geography
—Lifestyles
—Learning

American Revolution

—Causes and Effects
—Historical Figures

Westward Movement

—Transportation
—Geography
—Lifestyles
—Conflicts through 1815

The study of economics is integrated into the history units.

United States Government

—Origins and Workings of the Constitution

FIGURE A.2. "Calling All Bear Colonists!"

WE NEED A BEARTOWN CHARTER!!

WHEREAS Queen Anna has made it known to her subjects that there may be some LAND for bears to permanently establish a colony and

WHEREAS she is requesting draft charter documents which will convince her that the bears will engage in educational, productive and responsible learning and

WHERAS Room 203 is fast becoming too small for bears to both engage in commerce AND build homes

PLEASE SUBMIT to a common meeting of your fellow bears on Friday, April 13th, a draft CHARTER for possible approval. The CHARTER must take into account educational goals and objectives of Queen Anna and her duly elected governmental representatives as outlined in the attached Grade 5 Curriculum.

Bears, you should know that other colonies have done this before you and that their charters still exist. One is attached for your reference. You may look at more charters of other colonies by visiting the website:

www.yale.edu/lawweb/avalon/states/charter_002

Your charter should be at least two hand-written pages. Queen Anna would like to know:

What you might need in order to meet the attached standards
How you will go about doing that as bears
How you will regularly inform her of your progress and
What products, goods, services she and her kingdom can expect
    from this bold and heretofore unchartered educational
    territory.

Your Faithful Servant,
Sweet Bear

Figure A.3. Homework for Beartown

Preparing a Circuit for Wiring My Beartown Home/Business

Remember Kevin's example of the light switch and bulb? If you want one of those for your home or business, please follow these easy directions.

1. Decide where you want to put your light bulb. Mark the spot (LB) with a pencil.
2. Decide where you want to put your switch. Mark the spot with an S for switch.
3. Decide where you want to put your battery holder. This one is a bit tricky. The dimensions of the battery holder are approximately 2" by 1" by ½" (height). Where it goes will have an impact on the way your bear home looks. Some people may want to "hide" it in a cabinet or under a bed. Wherever the battery holder goes, it will have to be accessible so you can change your batteries whenever that is needed. Make an outline of the battery holder dimensions in pencil once you have decided where it will go.
4. Make a light line, in pencil, that connects the light bulb, switch, and battery holder. This is where your wiring will be going. Consider putting the wiring in a place that will not be noticed or in a place that you can decorate over easily with contact paper, electrical tape, or some other "wallpaper" you will be using.
5. Meausure the total amount of wire you will need.
6. Bring this paper in on Monday with numbers 1–5 above done and checked off and the sentences below filled out.

I will need _____ inches of wiring for my light fixture.

(Check one below)

____ I do not need any additional light fixtures.
____ I would like a second light fixture. Here is $6.00 to pay for the materials for my second light fixture.

Name: _____   Parent Signature: _____

FIGURE A.4. Beartown Information Sheet

Dear Colleagues,

As many of you have noticed, Beartown is under construction in the courtyard. It will be ready for viewing and using by other classrooms on Festival Day which will be Thursday, June 14th. The entire day will be taken up with Beartown visits. A sign-up sheet is on the back counter.

What we envision (and this could be tweaked for any visiting class) is classes coming with their bears to the LIBRARY entrance to Beartown. Owners of bears will be given a little coin envelope with some Beartown money (play money from Ms. K. as well as one or two Beartown dollar bills). Students will first be able to tour Beartown homes and talk with their builders (about 15 mins. or so). Then, they can come to Main Street where they can shop for various bear items that have been lovingly created by the Beartown shop keepers. Some items include: accessories for the bears, clothing for the bears, sports equipment, paper guitars, paper cars, fast cash banking cards, health club membership cards, restaurant gift certificates, tavern menus, etc. If you want to come, please sign up your class for a half-hour slot. There is no rain date planned. We are just praying desperately for good weather. Please join us in this prayer effort!!!

We also have a Beartown website, complete with biographies of our bears. Please visit it at: freewebs.com/beartownunited. We would be happy to create a link on the website for classrooms who have, or would like to create, biographies and/or brief information about their individual bears for public viewing. (I have been able to speak to some of the third and second grade teachers about this but some of you I have not.) Please send the biographies to room 203 as soon as they are ready. We will send a message to you when they have been put up on the website.

Thank you so much for your interest in Beartown!!! We are thrilled to be able to provide this service to the Miller School community!

Bear-Focused Children's Books

Ache, Frank. (2001). *Good Night Baby Bear*. New York: Harcourt.

Aylesworth, Jim. (1997). *Teddy Bear Tears*. New York: Atheneum.

Butler, Dorothy. (1988). *My Brown Bear Barney*. New York: Greenwillow.

Castle, Caroline. (2007). *Brown Bear's Wonderful Secret*. London: Pinwheel.

Collier, James Lincoln. (2001). *The Teddy Bear Habit*. New York: Hyperion Books.

De Beer, Hans. (2004). *The Secret Hide Out: A Little Polar Bear Story*. New York: Sterling.

Dematon, Charlotte. (2004). *Worry Bear*. Honesdale, PA: Boyds Mill Press.

Fox, Mem. (2002). *Sleepy Bears*. New York: Harcourt Trade.

Freeman, Don. (1968). *Corduroy*. New York: Viking.

Freeman, Don. (1980). *A Pocket for Corduroy*. New York: Penguin.

Hachler, Bruno. (2004). *What Does My Teddy Bear Do All Day?* London: Penguin.

Howe, Deborah & James. (1994). *Teddy Bear's Scrapbook*. Bel Air, CA: Sagebrush Education.

McClosky, Robert. (1948). *Blueberries for Sal*. New York: Viking.

McPhail, David. (1990). *Lost*. Boston: Little, Brown.

McPhail, David. (2002). *The Teddy Bear*. New York: Henry Holt & Company.

Minarik, Else Holmelund. (1957). *Little Bear*. New York: HarperCollins.

Plourde, Lynn. (2007). *Pajama Day*. New York: Penguin.

References

Beebe, B. (2004). Faces in relation, a case study. *Psychoanalytic Dialogues, 14*(1), 1–51.

Drucker, J. (1994). Constructing metaphors: The role of symbolization in the treatment of children. In A. Slade & P. W. Dennie (Eds.), *Children at play* (pp. 62–80). New York: Oxford University Press.

Friedman, D. (2005). *Interaction and the architecture of the brain.* Washington, DC: National Scientific Council on the Developing Child. Retrieved July 7, 2006, from http://www.developingchild.net/papers/020705_interactions_article.pdf

Gibson, E. J., & Walk, R. D. (1960). The "visual cliff." *Scientific American, 202*(4), 67–71.

Gunnar, M. (2003). Integrating neuroscience and psychosocial approaches in the study of early experiences. In J. A. King, C. F. Ferris, & I. I. Lederhendler (Eds.), *Roots of Mental Illness in Children, 1008* (pp. 238–247). New York: New York Academy of Sciences.

Hamre, B. K., & Pianta, R. C. (2001). Early teacher-child relationships and the trajectory of children's school outcomes through eighth grade. *Child Development, 72*(2), 625–638.

Jaffe, S. A. (2007). Sensitive, stimulating caregiving predicts cognitive and behavioral resilience in neurodevelopmentally at-risk infants. *Development and Psychopathology, 19*(3), 631–647.

Koplow, L. (2002). *Creating schools that heal: Real-life solutions.* New York: Teachers College Press.

Koplow, L. (2007). *Unsmiling faces: How preschools can heal.* New York: Teachers College Press.

Meltzoff, A. N., & Decety, J. (2003, March 29). What imitation tells us about social cognition: A rapprochement between developmental psychology and cognitive neuroscience. *Philosophical Transactions: Biological Sciences, 358*(1431), 491–500.

National Scientific Council on the Developing Child at Harvard University [NSCDC]. (2005). *Excessive stress disrupts the architecture of the brain* [Working Paper #3]. Retrieved July 15, 2006, from http://www.developingchild.net/reports.shtml

National Scientific Council on the Developing Child at Harvard University [NSCDC]. (2007). *The science of early childhood development: Closing the gap between what we know and what we do.* Retrieved June 5, 2007, from http://www.developingchild.net

Nicolopoulou, A., McDowell, J., & Brockmeyer, C. (2006). Narrative play and emergent literacy: Storytelling and story-acting meet journal writing. In D. G. Singer, R. Golinkoff, & K. Hirsh-Pasek (Eds.), *Play = learning: How play motivates and enhances children's cognitive and social-emotional growth* (pp. 124–144). New York: Oxford University Press.

Paley, V. G. (2004). *Importance of fantasy play.* Chicago: University of Chicago Press.

Shonkoff, J., & Phillips, D. A. (2000). *From neurons to neighborhoods.* Washington, DC: National Academy of Sciences.

Watamura, S. E., Donzella, B., Alwin, J., & Gunnar, M. R. (2003). Morning to afternoon increases in cortisol concentrations for infants and toddlers at child care: Age differences and behavioral correlates. *Child Development, 74*(4), 1006–1020.

Winnicott, D. W. (2005). *Playing and reality.* New York: Routledge. (Original work published 1971)

Children's Books Cited

Anastos, Ernie. (2008). *Ernie & The Big Newz*. New York: New World Books.

Anholt, Catherine. (2002). *Billy and the Big New School*. Morton Grove, IL: Albert Whitman.

Averill, Esther. (2005). *The School for Cats*. New York: NYR Children's Collection.

Barnes, Derrick. (2008). *Brand New School*. New York: Scholastic.

Berry, Vera Rosen. (2006). *Vera's New School*. New York: Henry Holt.

Bonsall, Crosby. (1999). *The Case of the Hungry Stranger*. New York: HarperCollins.

Bonsall, Crosby, & Lewis, E. B. (1984). *The Case of the Scaredy Cats*. New York: HarperCollins.

Brown, Jeff. (2003). *Stanley and the Magic Lamp*. New York: HarperCollins.

Curtis, Jamie Lee. (1993). *When I Was Little*. New York: HarperCollins.

Friedman, Carol. (2005). *Nicky the Jazz Cat*. Brooklyn, NY: Powerhouse Books.

Givner, Joan. (2006). *Ellen Fremedon: Journalist*. Toronto: Groundwood Books.

Hains, Harriet. (1992). *My New School*. New York: DK Publishing.

Hammonds, Heather. (2003). *When Grandpa Was Young*. Southbank, Victoria, Canada: Thomson Nelson.

Harris, Robie H. (2003). *I Am Not Going to School Today*. New York: McElderry Books.

Heidbreder, Robert. (2000). *I Wished for a Unicorn*. Toronto: Kids Can Press.

Henkes, Kevin. (1988). *Chester's Way*. New York: Greenwillow.

Polanco, Patricia. (1991). *Appelemando's Dream*. New York: Penguin.

Scieszka, Jon. (1995). *The Time Warp Trio, 2095*. New York: Penguin.

Taulbert, Clifton L. (2001). *Little Cliff's First Day of School*. New York: Dial.

Thomas, Pat. (2006). *Do I Have to Go to School?* Happauge, NY: Barron's Educational Series.

Vaccaro, Laura. (2007). *First the Egg*. New York: Roaring Brook.

For Further Reading

Beebe, B., & Lachmann, F. (1998). Co-constructing inner and relational processes: Self- and mutual regulation in infant research and adult treatment. *Psychoanalytic Psychology, 15*(4), 480–516.

Gunnar, M. R., & Donzella, B. (2002). Social regulation of the cortisol levels in early human development. *Psychoneuroendocrinology, 27*, 199–220.

Hamre, B. K., & Pianta, R. C. (2005). Can instructional and emotional support in the first-grade classroom make a difference for children at risk of school failure? *Child Development, 76*(5), 949–967.

National Scientific Council on the Developing Child at Harvard University [NSCDC]. (2004). *Young Children Develop in an Environment of Relationships.* Working Paper No.1. Retrieved March 25, 2008, from http://www.developingchild.net

Index

About the Author

Lesley Koplow, M.S., L.C.S.W., is the Director of the Center for Emotionally Responsive Practice at Bank Street College in New York City. The Center works with schools, agencies, and early childhood centers to support the emotional and social development of children from preschool through the elementary school years. Ms. Koplow is also a psychotherapist in private practice, a speaker/ presenter, and a consultant on child mental health issues. She lives in Manhattan with her daughter and their two cats. She has written several other books, including *Unsmiling Faces: How Preschools Can Heal* and *Creating Schools That Heal: Real-Life Solutions*, both published by Teachers College Press.